There's Got to be More!

Connecting Churches & Canadians

Reginald W. Bibby

With a foreword by
Carl S. Dudley

Wood Lake
Books
1995

Cover design: Lois Huey Heck
Editing and page design: Jim Taylor

Canadian Cataloguing in Publication Data

Bibby, Reginald W. (Reginald Wayne), 1943—
There's got to be more! Connecting Churches & Canadians

Includes bibliographic references
ISBN 1-55145-048-8

1. Church and the world. 2. Mission of the church.
3. Canada—Religious life and customs. I. Title
BR115.W6B52 1995   161'.1'0971   C95-910188-8

Published in Canada by
Wood Lake Books Inc.
10162 Newene Road
Winfield, BC V4V 1R2

Printed in Canada by
Hignell Printing Ltd.
Winnipeg, MB R3G 2B4

Contents

Preface

This book is anything but a solo effort.

The research on which it is based, spanning the early 1970s to the present, has been made possible by a number of generous funding sources—the Social Sciences and Humanities Research Council, the United Church of Canada, the Canadian Youth Foundation, and the University of Lethbridge. The Lilly Endowment, directly and through the Louisville Institute for the Study of Protestantism and American Culture, has given the research program significant support since 1990. Close to 20,000 adults and teenagers have taken the time to participate in the national and denominational studies.

Then there have been innumerable individuals and groups who, because of their interest in the findings and implications for ministry, have provided much stimulation. They include Brian Stiller, Bud Phillips, Jim Wallace, George Egerton, Don Bastian, Doug Hall, Armand Mauss, Clark Pinnock, Kirk Hadaway, Brian Fraser, Maxine Hancock, Clark Roof, Brian Aitken, Don Posterski, Aziz Khaki, Penny Marler, Benton Johnson, Jim Savoy, and James Penner. I particularly thank those people who, in the last year, have helped in assessing some of the ideas in this book—including the class at McMaster in the summer of 1994, the Baptist national staff in Ottawa, the Oblate Fathers in Edmonton, and the United Church leaders in Winnipeg brought together by Earl Gould.

I apologize that more people with helpful ideas could not be included in Chapter 7. Among the most prominent is Carl Dudley, who wrote the foreword to this book.

An individual whose observations a few years back were of central importance in encouraging me to look more closely at the receptivity to ministry of Canadians is Gordon Legge of *The Calgary Herald*. It's no accident that the research has become well-known. Gordon, along with a number of writers and broadcasters—notably, Bob Harvey, Doug Todd, Tom Harpur, Michael Valpy, Harvey Shepherd, Michael McAteer, Jack Kapica, David Roberts, Leona Flim, Virginia Byfield, Harold Jantz, Ann Petrie, Peter

Gzowski, Michael Enright, Bill Good, Ron Collister, and Andy Barry—have done much to make the work available to Canadians over the past two decades.

As always, I thank my family—especially Reggie, Dave, Russ and Jo—for their support, along with The University of Lethbridge.

In my mind, it's most appropriate that this book is being published by Wood Lake Books. Jim Taylor was there in the beginning when the United Church, led by Dave Stone, Howie Mills, and Clarke MacDonald—stuck its neck out and provided the first $2,000 for that pioneering 1975 Survey. And if you not only comprehend but actually enjoy what I've written, give some credit to Ralph Milton, who once told me, "You do a better job than 95% of academics in writing stuff that people can understand. But you've got to do better!"

—Reginald W. Bibby
Lethbridge, February, 1995

Dedication

To my Dad,
Reginald E. Bibby

*who lived his life
for family and faith*

Foreword
by Carl S. Dudley

Reginald Bibby faces the harsh realities of declining church membership and sees fresh possibilities. As an internationally respected Canadian-based social analyst who cares deeply about the Christian faith, he writes his book more like a news reporter than a sociologist. With solid statistical support he documents the crisis, and yet believes that churches are "uniquely positioned" to act. But he does not try to save the churches for their own sake. Rather he shows how churches that engage in Christian mission of spiritual nurture and human care may, in the act of reaching others, themselves be restored to life.

Bibby is known in the United States for excellent research, clear insights into religious and social change, and memorable metaphors that capture the essence of complex issues. Images from his earlier works *Fragmented Gods* and *Unknown Gods*, phrases such as "religion à la carte," have become standard in sociology of religion to describe the spirit of individual choices in the new ethos of the religious marketplace. His analysis and recommendations for Canadian churches have become foundational for American work as well.

But this book is different. Bibby shows more clearly the meaning of Canadian statistics, not just for analytical trends but action in the churches—at least for those leaders who accept the challenge. This is no book for avoidance Christians, for church members who cling to the past, for leaders who want easy answers. With irrefutable information from many resources, Bibby eliminates our favorite ways of blaming others in order to avoid our own responsibilities. After discussing numerous cultural and contextual shifts that have been hard on churches, Bibby cuts to the nub: the church is the problem.

With the same unflinching honesty, he offers churches new hope. He invites church leaders to see the world differently—not insiders vs. outsiders, not members vs. non-members. Rather he points to concentric layers of people who have an affinity with each particular religious group. He does not expect new strength in the churches from impossible sources (he names them), but from those on our doorsteps who are already inclined to care. He does not give answers, since each church must ultimately make its own decisions. But he does tell us where and how to look, what to look for, what technology we can use, and how to know when it is working.

Reading Bibby is like joining a highly energized conversation. Like a master teacher-coach, his banter is lively, and he anticipates our questions as his information unfolds. With notes and references to other publications for those who want more depth, he includes in our dialogue a wide variety of voices—from the prophetic witness of the Bible to the most current social research, from relevant computer technology to those personal experiences that we all have shared in attempting to empower local churches.

As his latest and most assertive book, *There's Got to be More* adds the "therefore" of actions to the implications of research that has been reported in previous books. Even (or especially) as he acknowledges the natural limitations of churches to appeal to everyone, he offers reasons for hope in particular directions that committed churches can attempt by knowing where we are and being who we are. Bibby offers not a spectator's analysis but an invitation to see the world differently, and to act on what we see with a real chance to seize this moment of unparalleled opportunity.

—Carl S. Dudley

Dr. Carl S. Dudley is Professor of Church and Community and Co-Director of the Center for Social and Religious Research of Hartford Seminary, in Hartford, Connecticut.

Introduction

I am writing this book because I believe that it needs to be written.

Paradoxically, at a time when numbers and morale are frequently sagging, cultural conditions in Canada point to an intriguing possibility: a great opportunity exists for the country's churches both to grow and expand the scope of their ministries. I want to do what I can to tell them to realize that opportunity.

The Canadian situation

We now know much about religion in Canada. We know much about the spiritual needs of individual Canadians, and we also know much about their relationship to organized religion. The picture the research has helped to clarify is extremely disturbing. I summed it up in this one blunt line in *Unknown Gods:* **"The churches are floundering at a time when they should be flourishing."**

The available research indicates that large numbers of Canadians—well beyond the 20 to 25% who regularly attend the nation's churches—are in need of the **God, self, society** themes that historically have been associated with religion. Put simply, a good number of people who are "unchurched" have spiritual, personal, and relational needs.

It is widely assumed that Canadians are no worse off for their increasing tendency to bypass the churches. According to most onlookers, they will simply look elsewhere to meet their God, self, and society needs. Nonchalant journalists presumptuously ask, "So where are people turning?" as if alternatives capable of picking up the slack were obvious and available.

Our findings to date, however, question such assumptions.

- **Spiritually**, many people, while not active in religious communities, continue to identify with churches and are reluctant to turn elsewhere; in the process, significant numbers are going hungry.
- **Personal needs**, notably the desire for positive self-esteem, the possibility of new beginnings, and life-stimulating hope, are frequently being inadequately met.
- **Interpersonally**, good relationships are elusive, while values that

make for social civility—such as generosity, honesty, and concern and respect for others—lack clear-cut proponents. Children who were exposed to Sunday schools, for example, at minimum were taught that they should be "kind" to other people; "kindness" isn't necessarily being intentionally taught anywhere outside of religious groups today.

In short, the decline in the participation in organized religion is showing signs of carrying with it some serious personal and social costs in Canada. Large numbers of people are not having central human needs met by the churches. But many also are not having those needs met by alternatives.

Frankly, I—along with more than a few observers—am not so sure that God cares all that much about what is happening to the churches. But I have little doubt that **God is more than a little concerned about the unmet needs of Canadians.**

The New Testament situation

In my travels, I have come across a number of religious leaders who are quick to claim God's endorsement of their ministries, reminding those who question what they are doing of the Apostle Paul's statement—that "Christ loved the Church and gave himself for it."

They should be more cautious. The Gospels show us a Jesus who had little use for the religious types of his day. This sociologist's rereading of those four New Testament books leaves me with some inescapable conclusions.

- In observing the visibly religious, Jesus harshly decried their widespread self-righteousness, their tendency to live out the letter rather than the spirit of the law, and their inclination to distance themselves from the very people who required ministry.
- Jesus himself ministered both in the synagogues and outside of them, mixing not only with devout people but also with so-called sinners, reminding his critics that he had come "to seek and to save that which was lost." He ministered to spiritual needs, forgiving sins and pointing people to God. But he didn't stop there.
- He actively addressed personal needs, feeding the hungry, healing the sick, even restoring life. He also gave considerable attention

to interpersonal life, teaching people how to relate with more compassion toward each other, particularly emphasizing the importance of such caring transcending immediate family, friendship, and racial boundaries, touching enemies, strangers, and outsiders as well.

The historical Jesus who didn't endorse synagogues just because they were synagogues should not be expected to endorse churches just because they are churches.

There is, in my thinking, good reason to believe that much that is taking place today in the name of "ministry" is fairly foreign to the concerns of Jesus. If the needs of Canadians are to be met, that has to change.

The great opportunity

For all their current problems, Canada's religious groups are well-positioned to respond to the times. That probably is an understatement: the fact of the matter is that they are undoubtedly "best-positioned" to speak to the spiritual and moral needs of the country. Individually and certainly collectively, religious groups possess the history, the institutional credibility, and the resources necessary to have a profound impact on Canadians and Canadian life. **Churches and Canadians, however, need to be better connected.**

Now let's be clear about a few things. I'm well aware that some people out there aren't all that troubled about the fact that church attendance and church participation are down. I—like you—know full well that some observers argue that the numbers situation reflects

a) the post-Christian era in which we are living,
b) the fact that the church is whittling itself down to a faithful remnant, and
c) the price that churches must pay for taking tough stands on tough issues.

It also might interest some readers to know that Bibby's end-in-all is not to get people back to church. My interest in understanding the magnitude and meaning of dwindling numbers is also not motivated by a simple-minded desire to return to some kind of nostalgical "golden age"—allegedly sometime in the pre-1960s—when pews were packed and souls being saved. My concern goes much deeper.

Empty pews and empty lives

Yes, I am troubled about declining numbers, but for two reasons seldom acknowledged by critics:

- From an organizational point of view, **numerical declines represent declines in resources.** It's not just that the pews are empty; religious groups have less human and financial resources with which to engage in ministry—regardless of how they conceptualize "ministry." Efforts to bring about social change or respond to personal needs do not come any cheaper than efforts to evangelize the country. Further, effectiveness in influencing government and television networks, for example, is closely tied to the votes and viewers that religious groups potentially represent. Declining numbers translate into declining social influence.
- From the point of view of ministry, the fact that the number of participants is down signals a harsh reality: **the spiritual, personal, and social needs of an increasing number of people are not being met by the churches**—and often by no other institution or source either. Those empty pews become a symbol of fragmented, empty lives.

The Christian faith historically has spoken of a God-driven concern for the individual, as well as of relationships that start with immediate ties and extend to community, country, and world. **The spiritual, personal, and social needs of Canadians should result in healthy religious groups expanding rather than contracting.** Empty pews raise the very real possibility that churches may not be in touch with the personal and social needs of Canadians.

In the light of such patterns of searching, receptivity, and need, this is not an era when churches should take pride in diminishing in size. These are times that call for growing churches and growing ministries.

Religion and research, Canadian-style

I frequently have cited sociologist Peter Berger's observation that **religious commitment involves commitment to clear perception.** Sound ministry needs to be informed by a clear reading of the people and culture in which it is taking place. Obviously, you can't launch a Ukrainian Orthodox ministry in a city with no Ukrainians. Less obvious is the futility of centering a ministry on worship in a subdivision where no one has any history or memory of worshiping.

Unfortunately, effective ministry in Canada has been hampered by the lack of good information. Up through the mid-1970s, much of the information we had on the religious beliefs and behavior of Canadians was impressionistic and anecdotal. National survey information was limited to occasional Gallup poll items asking people about attendance at church services, with some questions about their beliefs and practices. Even Gallup only began to systematically probe church attendance around 1955—some 15 years after the polling company appeared in Canada. It appears that only one national denominational survey was carried out in the pre-1970s— Stewart Crysdale's 1964 survey of United Church members, published one year later in *The Changing Church in Canada.*

Recognizing the need for better information on the religious characteristics of Canadians, I conducted the first comprehensive national survey of religion in this country. Entitled *Project Canada*, this pioneering survey launched what has evolved into an extensive and on-going religious research program. The program has centered around national adult surveys completed in 1975, 1980, 1985, 1990, and now 1995. These surveys were complemented by 1984 and 1992 national surveys of Canadian teenagers, in collaboration with Don Posterski. The youth surveys have further enhanced the monitoring of social trends, by making intergenerational comparisons possible.[1]

While the Project Canada findings have been widely disseminated in some 50 articles and five books,[2] a number of issues have emerged:

● The very mass of information generated from the research program has created a problem: people have difficulty isolating the key findings. The trees easily get lost in the forest of data. Little wonder that ministers who tell me how much they enjoyed reading *"Fractured Gods"* have problems keeping the ideas straight!

- Many readers have difficulty understanding the implications of the findings for ministry. It's one thing, for example, to learn that people are into religion à la carte or that they are fascinated with supernatural ideas; it's another thing to know what such findings mean for how ministry should be carried out.

- Even when the implications are recognized—such as the need to track geographically-mobile members or to utilize requests for rites of passage as an opportunity for ministry—it often is not as clear how such implications can be translated into practical efforts. Policy is still looking for practice.

Another issue is becoming increasingly important. In the course of trying to adjust to current conditions, many church leaders are turning to research done in other countries and other contexts. The most obvious choice is American research and, in particular, American "gurus" who are increasingly available both live and via video. They include Lyle Schaller, Carl Dudley, Loren Mead, Bill Easum, and Herb Miller. Models such as "Willow Creek" and techniques like "telemarketing" are being widely embraced. In addition to American leads, some groups are suggesting that we can learn much from the British experience.

As I have stressed in *Fragmented Gods*, however, religion in Canada is different in many ways from religion in either the United States or Britain. For one thing, the dominant groups are not the same—Conservative Protestants, for example, make up some 35% of the U.S. population and only about 8% of ours; Anglicans are the largest group in Britain while Roman Catholics are the largest group here. The "rules" are also very different between the three countries. American religion is characterized by a highly competitive and flamboyant "market," whereas Canadian religious groups tend to service their respective affiliates with minimal fanfare—somewhat simlar to the style of British religious groups.[3]

Such divergent participation patterns, rules, and resources suggest that we need to proceed with caution when moving research findings and programs across national borders. We can learn much about how to carry out ministry in Canada from the Americans and

British. We also can learn much about **how not** to carry out ministry in Canada from the Americans and British.

It seems to me that what is needed is for us to first understand what is happening in our own culture, and then draw selectively on those features of successful ministry elsewhere that we judge to be appropriate. Such is the approach I am taking in this book.

With that background behind us, "Let's"—as the British put it—"get on with it."[4]

Reluctance, Lutheran-Style

I remember a dance at our high school when I was in my early teens. The boys stood on one side of the gym and talked, nervously looking over at the girls who were standing on the other side of the gym doing the same thing. There was one girl in particular who caught my eye. The evening was winding down. Finally, with palms sweating and a mouth so dry that I was afraid that I would squeak when I spoke, I slowly and anxiously crossed the floor to where she stood. When I got there, I finally asked, "Will you dance with me?"—to the girl standing next to her.

I think that those feelings of anxiety and confusion just about sum up how most Lutherans feel about talking about their faith with other people. We know it's a good idea. We think it should come naturally. We even suspect that it might be a lot of fun if we could muster up the courage and go over there and say something. Much of the time we just think about it and somehow never cross the room.

—*Kenn Ward, Evangelical Lutheran Church in Canada*
pastor and journalist.[5]

*We speak of what we know
and we testify to what we have seen.*
—John 3:11

Chapter 1
The Ten Key Findings

I frequently come across people who tell me that they have "heard something" about my religion research, and then ask, "What have you found?" At first such a seemingly innocent question was somewhat annoying—after all, how does a person sum up 25 years of research in a few sentences? Increasingly, however, I have come to side with the person asking the question. There now is so much data and so many articles and books out there that I occasionally ask myself, "So, in short, what **have** you found?"

My initial response is, "A lot." The adult surveys since 1975, the teen surveys since 1984, the *Anglitrends* study of the Toronto Anglican Diocese in 1985 and the *Unitrends* national study of The United Church in 1994, the research on evangelicals in Calgary that began in 1971—those add up to a tremendous amount of information that represents a rich and invaluable resource for churches.

I consequently am committed to laying out the highlights with more clarity than ever before. So here's what I consider the **ten most important findings of my research for religious leaders.**

▌ Participation is down—sharply

Since at least the late 1940s, there has been a pronounced drop in weekly church attendance in Canada. The earliest poll data available, provided by Gallup for 1945, indicate that some 60% of the population maintained that they were attending services on close to a weekly basis at that time. The 60% figure fell to around 50%

by 1960, to about 30% by 1980, and now stands at just over 20%.

- Religious group differences are striking: the greatest decreases between the mid-50s and mid-90s have been experienced by the Roman Catholic Church in Quebec (from 90% attendance to 25%) and the United Church (from 40% to 20%).
- Roman Catholic attendance outside of Quebec has dropped significantly over the past four decades, yet still stands relatively high at about 40%.
- Conservative Protestant attendance has risen since the mid-70s, and now is the highest of any group, at close to 60%.

Church Attendance in Canada: 1957–1993
% indicating attending "almost every week" or more

	1957	1975	1993
Nationally	53	31	23
Roman Catholic	83	45	30
Outside Quebec	75	49	42
Inside Quebec	88	41	27
Anglican	24	24	16
United	40	28	20
Conservative Protestant	51	40	59

*Source: Bibby, Unknown Gods, 1993:4–6;
for 1993, Maclean's, April 12, 1993: 33ff.*

As service attendance has declined, so has personal religious commitment—although not to the extent of group involvement. In 1975, for example, some 65% of Canadians indicated that religion was very important to them. As of the 1990s, that figure has slipped to about 55%. The drop has been about 10 percentage points for both women (69% to 60%) and men (60% to 52%).

These trends are understandably disturbing to most religious leaders. **The fact of the matter, however, is that the worst is yet to come.** A simple analysis of current weekly attendance by age reveals that churchgoers are disproportionately old: weekly attenders come in at 37% for those 55 and over, 23% for people 35 to 54, and only 14% for those between the ages of 18 and 34.

It doesn't take a brilliant demographer to project the obvious: with the aging of the Canadian population over the next 20 years or so, a dramatic drop in attendance is going to take place—barring some equally dramatic, unforeseen developments.

- Many of today's 55-and-overs—the group most supportive of Canada's churches—will disappear from the scene.
- They will be replaced by current 35- to 54-year-olds, meaning the level of involvement for Canada's oldest churchgoing group will drop from almost 40% to about 25%.
- That middle-age group will be replaced by today's under-35 crowd—meaning involvement for 35- to 54-year-olds will decline from about 25% to a mere 15%.
- And, today's adults under 35 will be replaced by today's teenagers and their younger sisters and brothers—the group with possibly the lowest amount of exposure to organized religion in Canadian history.

It's not exactly a pretty projection. There is good reason to believe that **in only 20 years—by approximately the year 2015—the proportion of people attending weekly will drop from today's 23% level to around 15%.**

Translated into actual numbers of people, in just 20 years' time:
- Nationally, the number of weekly attenders will fall from today's 4.5 million to 3.5 million.
- Regular Roman Catholic churchgoers in Quebec will decline by one-half—from 1.2 million to 600,000.
- Anglican weekly attenders will drop from today's 220,000 to 100,000.
- The United Church will see its weekly attenders cut in half—from about 400,000 to 200,000.
- The mixed news for Roman Catholics outside of Quebec is that the Church will lose about 200,000 regular attenders, but will still have over 1 million people attending weekly—easily the most of any Canadian group.
- The most positive news is associated with Conservative Protestants, but it's not as positive as many people think: these evangelical groups will experience growth but it will be fairly modest. Evangelicals will add some 200,000 weekly attenders in the next two decades, bringing their weekly total to some 1.3 million peo-

17

ple. The downside is that this kind of growth will fall far short of the hopes of "Vision 2000," and may be seen as a failure.

By the year 2015, on an average Sunday, there will be three Canadians in a Conservative Protestant service for every one person attending United, Anglican, Presbyterian, and Lutheran services combined. Outside of Quebec, the Roman Catholic worshiping total will be about the same as that of the Conservatives.

Obviously there are some geographical and congregational exceptions to these national patterns—both positive and negative. All Mainline congregations are not declining, just as all Conservative Protestant congregations are not growing. Collectively, however, the news is not very good for Canada's religious groups.

2 Few people are actually leaving

The drop in weekly attendance has led many leaders to assume that people are literally being "lost" to the churches. If they are not showing up, the assumption is that, at best, they have dropped out and have simply become inactive. At worst, they have defected to some other group, possibly of the grassroots evangelical variety.

Most of the consternation about dropout and defection, however, is not warranted. As of the latest, 1991 census:

- some 8 in 10 Canadians continue to view themselves as Roman Catholics or Protestants—in 1871, the figure was about 9 in 10;
- only 4% of Canadians identify with other faiths—essentially the same as 50 years ago;
- while 12% of Canadians currently say that they have "no religion," many appear to be younger, "temporary nothings" who frequently will turn to religious groups for marriage and birth rites—often "reaffiliating" with their parents' religion in the process.
- intergenerational retention rates remain high:
  - approximately 90% of Canadians from Roman Catholic homes continue to identify with Roman Catholicism
  - 85% for Mainline Protestants (United, Anglican, Presbyterian, Lutheran)
  - 65% for Conservative Protestants ("evangelical groups" such as Baptist, Pentecostal, Salvation Army, Mennonite, Alliance, Nazarene, Reformed)

—and 75% for other faiths (such as Judaism, Islam, Hinduism, Buddhism).

Regardless of their participation levels in religious groups, Canadians are still including religion when they define themselves. They may not be showing up all that much. But they're still out there and they still are thinking that they are Roman Catholic, United, Anglican, Lutheran, Presbyterian, Baptist, Mennonite, Jewish, and so on. The more "historic" the faith group, the more likely it seems that people continue to define themselves by it.

Think I'm exaggerating? Frankly, I've considered that possibility myself. Consequently, one corrective I've tried to use is to tell people what I've had in mind, and ask them how well they recognize themselves in the descriptions I've been giving of them.

Specifically, in both the 1985 and 1990 national surveys, I asked Canadians who said that they are not regular churchgoers to respond to this statement:

Some observers maintain that few people are actually abandoning their religious traditions. Rather, they draw selective beliefs and practices, even if they do not attend services frequently. They are not about to be recruited by other religious groups. Their identification with their religious traditions is fairly solidly fixed, and it is to these groups that they will turn when confronted with marriage, death, and frequently, birth. How well would you say this observation describes YOU?

In both surveys,
- close to 90% of people who still identified with a religious group but were not attending regularly said that the statement described them either "very accurately" or "somewhat accurately";
- the "accuracy" figures were just over 90% for inactive Roman Catholic, United, and Anglican affiliates, and
- around 85% for inactive Conservative Protestants, Lutherans, and Presbyterians.

For all the alarm about defection, these findings suggest that the vast majority of Canadians are "still at home." As I have pointed out in *Unknown Gods,* even when groups would like to delete some of these inactive types from their membership rolls, the truth of the matter is that these people are hard to shed. They can be chastised, ignored, and removed from church lists—and they frequently are. But they don't really leave. Psychologically, emotionally, and culturally, they continue to identify with their religious traditions.

The research is decisive: **defection from the groups of one's parents is relatively uncommon.** People may not be highly involved in their groups. But most retain psychological and emotional ties.

3 Religion à la carte is rampant

Canadians are fussy customers. We have a wide range of choices in virtually every area of life. We can take our pick from an array of possibilities when it comes to day-to-day shopping, entertainment, education, medicine, finance, and politics, not to mention lifestyle, family structure, sexuality, and morality.

Simultaneously, we keep saying that we have two primary personal concerns: we don't think that we have enough money, and we don't think we have enough time.

The combination of unlimited choices on the one hand and the perception of limited resources on the other has resulted in people practicing **selective consumption**.

When Canadians as a whole turn to religion, they don't change their posture. They approach religion with the same "pick and choose" mentality that they show pretty much everything else. For starters, they attend when they want. But **sporadic attendance is merely the tip of the religion à la carte iceberg.**

Other results are familiar to church leaders: Canadians tend to accept "the party line" when it comes to believing in God, the divinity of Jesus, and life after death, but they essentially ignore teachings concerning sexuality, gambling, and capital punishment. People want some services that groups provide, notably rites of passage. But they frequently prefer to pass on preparation classes, Sunday schools, and study groups. And, of course, they are prepared to give religious groups only so much time and money. As one United Church board member in Calgary bluntly informed her colleagues in a consultation a few years back: "You people need to understand that I'm prepared to give this church two hours a week. If there's a board meeting on Wednesday night, don't expect to see me at church on Sunday morning!"

The selective consumption approach to much of Canadian life is not just the result of limited resources. **It has its roots in an accelerated amount of individualism.** As I have pointed out in some detail in *Mosaic Madness*, since the 1950s, there has been a growing tendency for people from British Columbia to Newfoundland to emphasize the individual over the group, or their group over the collectivity. The emphasis on the individual may have been important as a corrective to an excessive emphasis on the group in the pre-1960s. Still, as American sociologist Robert Bellah has pointed out in his book, *Habits of the Heart,*[6] individualism taken too far can make social life at all levels—relationships, family, community, nation, and world—extremely difficult. It's no accident that Canada has experienced considerable social fragmentation in recent years; individualism in excess can contribute to a socially debilitating style of "all for one and none for all."

Individualism has also been accompanied by an emphasis on relativism—the idea that "truth and right" exist only in the eye of the beholder. Make no mistake about it: relativism is pervasive. In 1990, the *Project Canada* national survey asked adults to respond to the statement, "What's right or wrong is a matter of personal opinion." Some 50% agreed. In 1992, among teenagers, the figure was considerably higher—65%. **External authority is out; personal authority is in.**

So Canadians interact with religious groups as fussy customers who want to pick and choose according to their consumption whims and personal sense of what is right. They tend to want only fragments of what the country's religious groups have to offer.

The problem is not that people seem to want so much; it's rather that they seem to want so little. Fragments are relatively unimportant consumer items, chosen over systems because they are more conducive to life in our present age.

4 Religion continues to be relational

There is little mystery as to why most people are involved in mainstream religious groups in Canada and elsewhere. **Religious involvement and commitment are learned like anything else. Relationships, led by the family, are religion's centrally important transmission lines.**[7]

- My ongoing research on evangelical churches in Calgary with Merlin Brinkerhoff, for example, has found that, to the extent that "outsiders" are recruited, they invariably come through friendship and marriage links with members.[8]
- It's no different for other groups. The 1994 *Unitrends* survey found that some 75% of today's active members in the United Church come out of United Church homes, with many of the remainder "marrying in."[9]
- Recent baby boomer research findings have provided some of the latest and strongest evidence of the strong tendency of parents to pass religion on to their children.[10]

Conversely, **disaffiliation also tends to have social sources.** People whose family members and friends are not involved tend to follow suit. A fairly reliable rule of thumb is this: "the devout beget the devout; the non-devout beget the non-devout."[11]

The research is conclusive for both conservative and mainline churches: **religious groups grow their own, primarily through their members' families.**

Such family sources of religious commitment are readily evident in Canada, whether we are looking at identification, attendance, or commitment. What's more, little has changed from the 1970s through the 1990s:

- Almost 90% of Canadians in 1975 and again in 1990 were identifying with the same Protestant, Catholic, Other, and None groupings as their parents, with little difference in the tendency to identify with the tradition of one's mother versus one's father.
- Over 80% of current weekly attenders in both 1975 and 1990 maintained that they had attended weekly when they were growing up, all but 5% accompanied by their mothers, 8 in 10 by both parents.
- About 85% of those who viewed themselves as "very religious" in 1975 indicated that their mothers also see themselves as very

devout; some 70% of those who were "very religious" said the same designation applied to their fathers.

● In both 1975 and 1990, attendance and commitment were highest for respondents whose mother and father attended weekly and were strongly committed.

Parents are playing the key source role in imparting participation and commitment. The old cliché that "young people represent religion's future" needs to be supplemented with a centrally important socialization point: parents are the key to the religious future of young people. Anyone who doubts such a conclusion needs only to reflect on the relationship between their faith and that of a mother or father—and the relationship, in turn between their faith and that of a son or daughter.

Intergenerational Identification: 1975, 1990 (in %s)				
	1975		1990	
	Women	Men	Women	Men
Identify with mother's religion	86	87	87	87
Identify with father's religion	88	87	82	86
Attended weekly as a child	86	81	81	81

Source: Project Canada *series.*

Precisely because religion is "transmitted" through significant relationships, Canadians—like people elsewhere—do not readily abandon the religions of their childhoods. And in those cases where they do, a relationship with someone—such as a friend or a marriage partner—is invariably involved.

This tendency for religious identification to be grounded in family and friendships brings us to religious memory.

5 Religious memory is everywhere

Almost 90% of adults and 80% of teenagers identify with one religious group or another. That's an important finding. At minimum, such identification means that **millions of Canadians—well be-**

yond the 20-25% who currently are weekly attenders—have psychological, emotional, and cultural ties with the country's religious groups.

Consider these additional fast facts concerning people who do not attend services regularly:

- Almost 80% say that they attended monthly or more when they were growing up; close to 7 in 10 were accompanied by their mothers, more than 5 in 10 by their fathers.
- Approximately one-half of those who don't attend on a regular weekly basis nevertheless say that both religion generally and their own religious group heritage specifically are "very important" or "somewhat important" to them; fewer than 1 in 5 indicate that they are "not important at all."

The cultures of those religious traditions include symbols such as family Bibles, family pianos, and family burial plots; in those cultures, we learn certain choruses and hymns, worship styles, language, theological ideas; we are exposed to particular role-models and lifestyles.

Canadians subsequently feel familiarity in certain religious cultures, and discomfort in others.

- A Protestant in a Roman Catholic service isn't sure what to do and when to do it.
- A Roman Catholic in a some Protestant services looks in vain for candles and statues, and wonders why the service ended without the Eucharist being celebrated.
- A journalist who has long since thrown over the evangelical faith of her childhood acknowledges that she finds herself wanting to cry when she hears the sounds of *Amazing Grace*—like Kris Kristofferson, she finds that it takes her "back to something that she lost somewhere, somehow along the way."[12]

Obviously those feelings are not always positive. For some, the religion of their parents may be associated with memories and emotions that are unpleasant, sometimes painful.

Yet, even among the disenchanted, what is "normal" in a religious sense is hard to shake. Many are inclined to view the ideas and styles of other religious groups through the eyes of the group in which they were raised. Accordingly, even in wedding and funeral situations, for example, these Canadians feel more comfortable or less comfortable with certain hymns and prayers, words and phrases, symbols and rituals.

Canadians who attend sporadically simply don't wake up on a given Sunday morning and make a random decision as to where they will catch a worship service. **They head in the direction of what is religiously familiar.**

In the 1990 national survey, we asked adults who do not attend services regularly where they or their children turn for occasional services or other activities, such as Sunday schools. We found that:

- 85% of inactive Mainline Protestants rely on Mainline churches;
- 76% of inactive Conservative Protestants turn to Conservative churches;
- 97% of inactive Roman Catholics look to Catholic churches.

The vast majority of Canadians continue to have psychological, emotional, and cultural links to their parents' religious groups. These links appear to be sustained not so much by religious content as by family history and rites of passage. This is why denominational walls are still in place, in both the United States and Canada, despite common claims to the contrary.

Because of the importance of the point, let me elaborate a bit. I'm well aware of the claims of people such as George Barna, Leith Anderson, and Lyle Schaller, along with Don Posterski and Irwin Barker, that denominations have lost much of their importance to people today.[13]

However, two issues have not been sufficiently resolved.

1. If one thinks not of denomination but of "religious families"— Mainline Protestants, Conservative Protestants, Roman Catholics, and Other Faiths—switching typically involves fairly short theological and cultural trips.

- While Dean Hoge and his associates, for example, have recently suggested that denomination is not very important to people who were raised as Presbyterians, their own data show that some 70% of their sample retained the "Presbyterian label" as adults.[14]
- Highly-regarded researchers Kirk Hadaway and Penny Marler have concluded that "the majority of church members [in the U.S.] never change denominations...when Americans do switch,

they often remain within the same broad denominational family."[15]

- Wade Clark Roof and William McKinney similarly have noted that, although at least 40% of American Protestants have switched denominations at one time or another, the figures for those remaining within "denominational families" come in at about 80% for Conservative Protestants and 70% for Mainliners. They maintain that such findings point to "levels of stability for the larger religio-cultural traditions in America today."[16]

- Consistent with U.S. findings, data collected by Don Posterski and Irwin Barker in 1992 on some of Canada's most active church members show that about 70% of current Mainliners and 65% of Conservative Protestants were raised in those "families." Further, less than 20% give denomination a "low" ranking as a factor to be considered when switching congregations.[17] My own research pegs the Roman Catholic retention level at almost 90%.[18]

2. Researchers might be confusing **tolerance zones** with **comfort zones**.

- Dean Hoge and his team have found that the tolerance zones of American Presbyterian baby boomers, for example, have expanded over the years, but personal comfort zones "are surprisingly narrow and traditional," extending for the great majority, "no further than mainline Protestantism" and for many, no further than Episcopalians![19]

- Similarly, the *Unitrends* national survey found that although about 95% of United Church members say they would feel comfortable in an Anglican worship service, the figure drops to 70% for a Roman Catholic mass, and 35% for a Pentecostal service.

Some of you are undoubtedly saying, "But I know for a fact that there are people in my congregation who come from other traditions." Maybe. Or maybe not.

First, ask yourself if their previous group was actually **outside, not just your denomination, but also your "religious family"**—Mainline Protestant, Conservative Protestant, or Roman Catholic?

Second, **don't assume that current involvement means that**

a permanent switch has taken place. People may attend a given church for highly practical purposes, such as location, children, friendships, a minister, and so on. Some Roman Catholics, hurt by their church's attitude to women priests or to divorce, may be attending the local United Church. That's not to say that they have switched their affiliation. They're "just attending somewhere." If the home church changes, these temporary residents may well move back.

The distinction is more than an academic one. If people feel no lasting attachment to a denomination or faith "family" beyond a given congregation, their "fickleness" has important implications for their future involvement in the denomination. Their apparent "switch" may be only a temporary stopover, en route back to the group of their childhood.

As of the '90s, this pattern of "involvement without actual identification" characterizes:

- only about one in 50 people who worship in Roman Catholic churches,
- one in four who attend Mainline Protestant congregations,
- and one in three people who attend Conservative Protestant churches.

Religious memory typically has strong family roots. As such, it is not easily erased.

Receptivity to spirituality is extensive

Ironically, precisely at a time when interest and involvement in organized religion seems to be hitting unprecedented lows, there is considerable evidence to suggest that fairly large numbers of Canadians are highly receptive to the very things that religion historically has addressed.

People across the country—both young and old—continue to be intrigued with mystery. Many have experiences that call for answers that often are not readily available.

- Some 50% think that they have personally experienced an event before it has happened (precognition).
- About 40% believe that we can have contact with the spirit world.

- More than 90% find themselves asking what happens after we die; 1 in 4 adults and 1 in 3 teenagers think that they themselves will be reincarnated.
- Over 80% maintain God exists, but there's more: some 45% of adults and 35% of teens maintain that they themselves have experienced God. And remember, for the teenagers, that's only "so far"; they haven't even hit 20 yet!

Such beliefs and experiences suggest that significant numbers of Canadians who are not involved in the churches are anything but closed to the mysteries of life and death.

Canadians also indicate that they are searching for meaning. It's not necessarily an everyday, pressing thing. But, from time to time—perhaps when facing a birth, an illness, or the death of a relative or friend, perhaps when coming to grips with a career or marital change, maybe when hitting "a decade birthday" of 30 or 40, 50 or 60, the questions are raised.

- Nine in 10 people say they find themselves asking questions such as "What is the meaning of life?" "Why is there suffering in the world?" and "How can I find real happiness?"
- Some 50% report that the question of life's meaning and purpose is something that concerns them "a great deal" or "quite a bit."
- About 80% or more indicate that they anticipate turning to religious groups for ceremonies relating to birth, marriage, and death. Sure, some are responding to family pressures and tradition, and are in reality customers shopping for churches with wide aisles and air-conditioning. But, as many a minister has reminded me over the years, at least some of these people have a sometimes poorly articulated sense—yet a sense nonetheless—that "God needs to be brought in" on these events.
- Although fewer than one in five teenagers attend services regularly and only 10% say that they place a high value on religious involvement, about 25% report that spirituality is very important to them, and 60% explicitly acknowledge that they have spiritual needs.

Organized religion may be in trouble; but large numbers of Canadians who are not highly involved in the churches show a remarkable openness to the supernatural and to spirituality.

Given the reality of selective consumption, the obvious question that arises is "how much" and "what kind" of religion do Canadians want... and need?

The "consumer report" I offered in *Fragmented Gods* about fussy customers seems to fly in the face of those who maintain that religion should speak to all of one's life. But then again, maybe not. Perhaps an important reason why people "pick and choose" is because they aren't sure what the churches have to offer. Maybe some people aren't aware that some of their interests and needs can be addressed by the churches.

Equally serious, **it may well be that the groups themselves have incomplete menus.** Their ministries do not provide a balanced emphasis on God, self, and society.

Perceptions of spirituality

"When you think of someone who is genuinely spiritual, how important do you consider the following characteristics to be?" (% indicating "Very Important" or "Somewhat Important")

Living out one's faith in everyday life	78
Having a basic knowledge of one's faith	76
Believing in a supernatural being or higher power	69
Raising questions of purpose and meaning	69
Engaging in private prayer	69
Struggling to find a faith to live by	64
Engaging in public practices such as worship services	59
Spending time with people who have similar beliefs	54
Telling others about one's beliefs	46
Experiencing the supernatural	26

Source: Project Canada Survey *series*

---

7 Most people are not looking for churches

I find that church leaders are often preoccupied with the question, "What will it take to get people back in the churches?" It's the wrong question to ask.

The research is clear: **the majority of Canadians are not in the market for churches.**

- Only about 20% of adults and teenagers attend every week—and the level is dropping.
- When it comes to sources of enjoyment, religious group involvement is ranked last nationally by both young people and adults.

Canadians are also not "in the market for religion."
- While interest in meaning and mystery is widespread, only about 25% of adults and 15% of teenagers say that they place a high value on "religion" as such.
- The teen research, for example, finds over and over that young people express an openness to things spiritual and disinterest in things organizational.[20]

Canadians are, however, in the market for the things that religion historically has been about.
- They are more than interested in "a product" that speaks to the unexplained and the unknown by offering answers that lie beyond the human plane. They are open to—in fact, are fascinated by— explanations of a supernatural variety.
- They are trying to make sense of what life is for, and to find out how to make their own existence more meaningful. Many find that their lives do not add up to particular significance.
- One in three explicitly acknowledge that they should be getting more out of life.
- Canadians also want to feel good about themselves, to have solid self-esteem and a sense of personal worth; they want to be able to minimize personal strain and pain, experience happiness and fulfillment, new beginnings, and life-invigorating hope.
- And besides staying alive and living well, there is nothing that Canadians young and old say they value more than good relationships. They want to love and be loved, and to experience good ties with the people they associate with.

No, most Canadians are not looking for churches—or religion. **But they do express spiritual, personal, and social needs.** Therein lies religion's "great opportunity." It's almost an ideal match-up...
- Canadians indicate that they have spiritual needs; the churches have much to say about God and spirituality.
- Canadians indicate that they have personal needs; the Judeo-Christian tradition, for example, says much about personal dignity and

fulfillment, resources and joy, new beginnings and hope.
- Canadians indicate that they have social and relational needs; a religion like Christianity attempts to teach people how to experience optimum relationships that start with family and friends and extend to outsiders, to the enhancing of social life regionally, nationally, and globally.

Unfortunately, "the obvious connection" often is not taking place.

Many observers assume, in a naive, matter-of-fact manner, that if increasing numbers of Canadians are not having their spiritual, personal, and relational needs met by the country's religious groups, they must be having them met in other ways. Academics, for example, have spoken of "privatized faith," while the media have given considerable attention in the post-1950s to a variety of new religious expressions. *Maclean's* devoted a front cover story to "The New Spirituality," with writer Marci McDonald telling the nation that "a massive quest for a new spirituality [is] currently gripping mainstream North America," and proceeded to discuss how it possibly is being met—everywhere but in traditional churches.[21]

The research to date, however, provides little evidence that Canadians who are no longer turning to the churches for needs pertaining to God, self, and society are automatically turning elsewhere.
- While some are curious about new religious ideas and may explore and adopt some New Age offerings, for example, most are extremely reluctant to abandon their traditional religions. The result is that large numbers of people are failing to have their spiritual needs met.
- Personal issues such as the need for positive self-esteem, new beginnings, and hope for better things have been central religious themes; but they appear to remain elusive goals for many Canadians. While self-worth, forgiveness, and hope can be instilled without religion's help, religion nonetheless has been an important ally whose contribution is being sorely missed.
- Interpersonally, the churches have at minimum aspired to and encouraged values such as compassion, generosity, and respect. It is not at all clear that the task of instilling such basic civility values has been assumed by any alternative source such as school, media, or home.

No, Canadians are not looking for churches. But there is good reason to believe that they continue to be very much in need of the God-self-society themes that churches are about.

Quest in search of God

Novelist Don DeLillo's bestseller *Mao II* characterizes our culture as crowded with lonely, isolated individuals and controlled by religious cults and terrorist groups. The book begins with a mass marriage of thousands of young couples by the Reverend Sun Myung Moon, leader of the Unification Church. The event actually occurred in Madison Square Garden in 1982. In DeLillo's account the stadium is filled with anxious, confused parents straining to identify a son or daughter in the swirling mass of anonymous couples. One father muses over the event and reflects: "When the Old God leaves the world, what happens to all the unexpended faith?"

For many, the "Old God" has left the world, but faith and the need to believe have not disappeared. So unexpended faith is swirling about looking for somewhere to root itself, some new "god" to satisfy its hunger. The church is not seen as a credible alternative.

—*Alan Roxburgh, minister and former director of the Center for Mission and Evangelism at McMaster Divinity College.*[22]

---

8 Most churches are not looking for people

It's not easy to say it, but it needs to be said: the research suggests that **one of the main reasons why Canada's churches are not ministering to a larger number of people is because they typically wait for people to come to them.**

Look at the data:
- More than 80% of today's weekly attenders were, in fact, attending that often when they were growing up; just 4% of the people who were attending "yearly or less" now are attending regularly.
- As many as seven in ten additions to congregations are active members of the congregations in the same "denominational families." Two in ten are the children of members, and only about one in ten have come from other religious families. When outsiders do appear, friendship and marriage seem to be the key links.
- Canada's religious groups continue to have considerable cultural homogeneity: some 85% of Anglicans, along with 80% of United

Church and Presbyterians, still have British roots; about 85% of Lutherans come from a limited number of European countries.[23]

● Many congregations and denominations appear to exist primarily to provide services for their active members; consistent with such an argument, congregations, for example, tend to "rise and fall" in accordance with their attractiveness to members who change residences.

Sources of additions to congregational membership

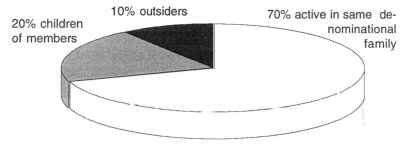

20% children of members

10% outsiders

70% active in same denominational family

I've maintained in *Unknown Gods* that, from an outsider's point of view, many religious groups look very much like "religious clubs," with fairly predictable clienteles and cultures.

If you have any doubts about such conclusions, do what I occasionally do—randomly attend the services of a variety of congregations. You'll discover the troubling reality almost everywhere. **Many churches function as if they are oblivious to the possibility that a stranger could be present.** They call people by first names. They discuss finances. They show no respect for the clock. Of course, if one assumes that only the initiated are present, there's no need to use surnames, to play down dollar problems, or to worry about punctual starting and closing times.

The problem I personally have with "the club" concept is that such churches run the risk of failing to reach out beyond the initiated, in terms of either membership or ministry. Homogeneous churches are not especially appealing to outsiders who, because of ethnicity or class or religious culture, do not "fit in."

But there's still more that needs to be said. **It's not at all clear that outsiders are always wanted.** As one United Church minister put it in a recent conversation with me, "People in my congregation say that they want more members. If they were really being honest, what they'd say is that they want more money but not more members."

Overly harsh? Perhaps. Still, ethnically, theologically, and culturally, a disturbing number of congregations and parishes constitute what amount to "religious clubs" and "family shrines." Their appeal to outsiders is limited, their enthusiasm for the uninitiated in question. In the pointed words of theologian Letty Russell, "Christian communities fear difference sufficiently that they usually spend a considerable amount of time tending the margins or boundaries of their communities, not in order to connect with those outside but rather to protect themselves from strangers."[24]

There's another way in which some churches have found themselves not looking for people. Ironically, some Mainline Protestant congregations have made a virtue of not recruiting people, celebrating their paucity of numbers. They pride themselves on being—to use a bit of business jargon—"lean and mean." Once in a while, they have even taken explicit shots at yours truly, relegating him to something of a—gulp—mindless bean-counter.

To minimize the reality of declining numbers is to minimize the more serious issue: **declining numbers suggest the very real possibility that fewer and fewer Canadians are having their spiritual, personal, and social needs met.** Muriel Duncan, the editor of *The United Church Observer,* puts things this way:

> Many of us are still repenting a history of forcing our beliefs on those with less power. So how do we now share our joy in Jesus in a just and positive way? Can we go humbly to those outside our churches...who are open to mystery? Can we open our churches to them so we can search together for answers and community, for faith?[25]

Many of Canada's churches are not doing a particularly good job of aiming their resources at Canadians who need to be involved and/or require ministry. Locked doors, inaccessible stairs, cold shoulders, and private gatherings too often send a less than subtle message to outsiders. The disparity between the needs of the population and the numbers touched by the churches suggests that far too many congregations are not "looking for people."

People not looking for churches, churches not looking for people. Those two realities sum up the tragedy of the current situation: **many Canadians are not associating their needs with the churches and many churches are not associating what they have with what Canadians need.** Churches and Canadians are badly in need of connection.

People who need to be reached

I recently read your book *Unknown Gods.* I am a member of that huge group of ex-church members you feature in your book—one of the Baby Boomers who withdrew from church life in utter confusion, at the age of 19. Apparently I have never been missed. Nevertheless, I cannot escape from the feeling that I AM a spiritual being, with spiritual needs.

I found myself wondering just what you could tackle as your next topic. Possibly you could look at WHY so many people have spiritual needs, but stay away from the churches. Could it be that my friends and I are not unusual, or abnormal, in feeling unwanted by, unwelcome at, and unacceptable to, Christian congregations? Maybe you would like to do some research and publish a book called, *Rejecting Gods,* for most of the people I know who are ex-church members seem to have experienced just that—judgmental attitudes, rejection, condemnation.

I am still confused by church teachings, still haunted by the questions, still yearning for answers that are useful to me.

—*A December, 1994 letter from a reader.*

 ## Part of the problem is culture

In retrospect, I think that *Fragmented Gods* drew our attention to a basic but very important point: **a major reason why Canadians respond the way that they do to organized religion is culture**. The sharp decline in church attendance since the 1940s is directly tied to the inclination to

- adopt a belief here and a practice there,
- want religion to speak to some areas but not others,
- resurface for baptisms, christenings, weddings, and funerals,
- not really come but not really leave.

In short, Canadians today tend to selectively draw items from increasingly diversified religious smorgasbords, reflecting broader cultural developments.

"Don't take it personally," was my message to clergy at the time. "What's happening to religion is happening in every other sphere of Canadian life. Selective consumption, pluralism, individualism, and relativism are being felt everywhere. Just ask retailers, or educators, or the media, or politicians."

There was and is much truth to such a position. There's no doubt about it: religion's effort to claim Canadians' time and money, beliefs and outlook, values and behavior, encountered some formidable competition in the late 20th century. Cultural developments, including the proliferation of choices, the increase in exposure to higher education, and the rise to prominence of electronic media as the major source of reality creation, have all had a dramatic impact on religion's role and influence.

Still, it would be a serious error to equate culture's impact on religion as totally negative. Culture is only partly to blame. To place undue emphasis on culture's negative role is to invite—it seems to me—at least three inappropriate responses.

1. Those who value faith can in effect **give up.** They can sit back and proclaim that the real problem is the era in which we live. Depending on their theological and historical outlooks, they will use phrases such as "last times" or "post-Christian era" or "post-modernism" to depict the bleak situation. After all, if it's culture's fault, it's not their fault. In fact, it's not apparent to such people that much can be done at all. It might be wise not to fight the inevitable too tenaciously, but rather accept the reality of the times and function as faithful remnants.

2. Perhaps worse, some might unconsciously **give in,** bowing to the selective consumption tendencies of the populace. Believing that "times simply have changed" and that "expectations have to be lowered," such people might make the organizational adjustments necessary to cater to à la carte-minded customers, further fragmenting the gods in the process.

3. Or they can **take too little** from culture—assuming that culture and its creators, including media, education, government, and business, have only a negative impact on religion. Here culture becomes something of an relentless enemy. This view overlooks the extent to which culture actually predisposes Canadians to religion, by stimulating, for example,
   - their interest in the supernatural,

- their quest for more fulfilling lives,
- their questions about living and dying, and about the possibility of healthy and satisfying relationships,
- the importance of justice and fairness, values and ethics.

In short, the problems of organized religion in Canada lie only partly with culture. Certainly culture defines the environment in which the churches "live and move and have their being." But that's only part of the story. Culture does not dictate the outcome of the game. Equally important—perhaps far more important—is how the churches themselves function in cultural environments.

⬛◯ The heart of the problem is churches

If the opportunity and need for ministry to larger numbers of Canadians is there, yet the number of people that are being touched by religious groups is actually decreasing, it's hard to escape the obvious conclusion: **churches today are collectively failing.** What makes the situation so disturbing is that they are failing at a time when conditions suggest that they should be flourishing.

Let's not mince our words: religious groups **are** organizations. If they are to function effectively, they have to operate as sound organizations. No one should act surprised to find that organizational efficiency makes efficient ministry possible, while organizational ineptitude makes ministry difficult.

We don't show such bewilderment when we reflect on the ups and downs of the corporate sector—be they Cadillac-Fairview or the Canadian Football League. When companies succeed or fail, we assume that such outcomes have something to do with their performances. We further assume that, even in difficult times, the best companies find ways to stay alive and even thrive. **Survival and success are not organizational accidents.**

If Canada's religious groups are not ministering to significant numbers of Canadians at a time when large numbers of people are exhibiting both openness and need, then a number of organizational questions need to be raised. In *Unknown Gods,* I focused on four lines of inquiry:

1. Structural issues

- Religious groups are typically top-heavy with volunteers. This can seriously jeopardize organizational efficiency. Perhaps insufficient attention is being given to optimum use of such unpaid workforces.
- Coordination between national bodies and local congregations appears to be a problem for many religious groups, frequently making the implementation of effective programs very difficult.
- Considerable attention and energy is devoted to ongoing issues relating to social and cultural change. These include considerations of the role of women, sexual orientation, worship practices, and theological reflections. In the process, large amounts of time and energy that could be used to minister to others are instead turned inward.
- The image of religious groups in Canada has been severely tarnished in the '80s and '90s by televangelist scandals, sexual abuse cases, and controversies over homosexuals and homosexuality. Further, women—in many instances—have continued to feel highly marginalized. The churches, in the eyes of many Canadians, are not associated with openness, generosity of spirit, and sheer joy. Such negative perceptions have made ministry to Canadians all the more difficult.

2. Product issues

Historically, religion has had much to say about three centrally important areas: **God, self, and society.** Ideally, the three themes are interwoven, with God first and foremost, giving the other two themes of self and society a unique tone.

- The finding that Canadians are fascinated with supernatural ideas, yet often don't associate that interest with the churches, suggests that the God emphasis is sometimes missing.
- Although many Canadians are searching for personal meaning, hope, and fulfillment, the fact that they frequently don't associate those kinds of quest with what the churches have to offer suggests that the combined God and self emphasis is not always readily apparent.
- Canadians young and old value nothing more highly than relationships. That they often don't associate enhanced social life— from immediate ties to global concerns—with what the churches have to offer suggests that the combined God, self, and society emphasis is not obvious in some settings.

3. Promotion issues

The three-dimensional product of God, self, and society is potentially powerful. But it is not at all clear that Canadians are aware of
that integrated "product."

- Many Canadians, looking at church buildings from the outside,
literally do not know "what they do in there." Architecture typically reveals little to the uninitiated onlooker—the guideline for
church signs, for example, seems to be "keep it inconspicuous."
Most churches in Canada are better known by the buildings, businesses, and parks around them than by what goes on inside.
- Advertising is usually limited to "the church pages," read by
"church people" who are looking for "their churches." It is not
exactly an ideal way to expand clientele.
- Efforts to "get the word out" to outsiders—through means such as
visitation and the distribution of brochures, books, and videos—
tend to take the largely outdated "total market approach," aiming
at the entire population. The results tend to be predictably poor.

Signs of the times

SIGN. An attention-getting device for the local church. Usually
presents to the public the name(s) of the resident clergy, the times of
worship, and the subject of last week's sermon. Signs are commonly
placed in highly visible locations, after which some church group or
other plants a bush or tree in front of them.

Andrew Jensen, GOD: (n) The Greatest User of Capital Letters.
A Modern Churchgoer's Dictionary, *Wood Lake Books, 1994:73*

---

4. Distribution issues

Groups that think they have something to offer Canadians who
express spiritual, personal, and social needs have to develop ways
of connecting with those people. They have to make sure that they
are getting "the product out of the warehouse to the customer."

- It seems clear that much alleged ministry to Canadians is being
done from the safety of sanctuaries.
- Ministry to the world, nation, and outsider is frequently delegated
to the denomination or "national church."
- Many congregations seem to have become ends in themselves.
They exist for each other, and become preoccupied with themselves and their way of "doing" religion. Lay ministry means nothing more than getting involved in running the church.

In sum, cultural conditions are making ministry in the '90s tough. But cultural conditions also are such that much can be done by well-run religious organizations.

Some critics invariably protest that I am overestimating both the need and the opportunity. Perhaps. But it surely is incumbent on those who value faith to do everything they can to respond, **before setting limits on what they can and need to accomplish.**

No, not everyone will respond to churches who seek to reach out and minister. Maybe, even with solid, well-planned efforts, the pool of people receptive to what the churches have to offer spiritually, individually, and relationally will turn out to be only 50% of the population, or perhaps 40%—maybe only 30%.

But my point is that **churches are well-positioned—indeed probably best-positioned—to respond to the central God-self-society requirements of Canadians.** And there's no doubt that the number of people who have such needs easily outnumbers the people who currently have contact with the churches. What is needed, and needed urgently, is for Canada's churches to do a much-improved job of making contact with Canadians and addressing their spiritual, personal, and social concerns.

As things stand, to the extent that religious groups are failing to respond to the needs at hand, the real losers are not the churches. The real losers are Canadians.

Change is needed. It also is possible. That's an understatement. The key pieces of the connection and ministry puzzle have been uncovered by the research. What is required now is the assembly.

*"Perplexed, they asked one another,
'What does this mean?'"*
—Acts 2:12

Chapter 2
The Five Crucial Implications

The Ten Key Findings point to the obvious general implication that religious groups have the opportunity of ministering to larger numbers of Canadians. But the findings also point to more specific implications, that involve looking at old things in new ways. Together they provide religious groups with the crucial pieces of the connection and ministry puzzle.

■ Think "Affiliate"

The first piece of the puzzle lies in the finding that Canadian religious groups continue to have large numbers of affiliates—people who identify with them. The sizes of these affiliate pools exceed any group's number of active members.

Consequently, to begin with, enhanced ministry to Canadians requires a major change in the way in which religious groups view people. It's time for religious groups to "lay claim" to their affiliates. An old reality needs to be seen through new glasses.

The old view maximized participation and minimized identification. If people didn't participate much, the conclusion was that their religious identification didn't mean much. They were assigned the derogatory terms of "drop-outs," "inactives," and "formers." They were periodically labeled as "deadwood"—often for financial rather than theological reasons, pruned from church rolls, and thrown into the religion dumpster.

Sound crass? Well, frankly, it often has been a crass process, not exactly consistent with New Testament stories about shepherds

spending endless hours looking for lost sheep, or gardeners pains-
takingly tending vines and fig trees until they bore fruit.

**The new view maximizes identification and minimizes partici-
pation.** It takes seriously the finding that Canadians, regardless of
how religious groups view them, continue to think that they are
United, Roman Catholic, Anglican, Baptist, Jewish, and so on. It
also takes seriously the finding that identification is typically associated with family history, and carries with it religious memory.
That memory has important implications for what people think is
normative when it comes to beliefs, practices, and church life, including worship.

It also has extremely important implications for "affinity
lines"—the groups with which they feel rapport.

"Thinking affiliate" means that virtually every Canadian is seen
as having a religious history; even most of the 12% of people who
claim no affiliation are viewed as having parents who identified
with a group. Only about 2% of Canadians can be considered "lifelong nones," neither identifying with a group themselves nor having parents with any affiliation.

The intensity and content of religious identification will differ considerably from person to person.

- Some affiliation lines are **tenacious**; people will have intense loy-
  alties to their identification groups. We all know people who are
  "Presbyterian," "Reformed," and "Alliance," for example, through
  and through. What's interesting is that these affiliation lines are
  not limited to people who are actively involved—individuals who
  would never dream of worshiping in a different church, parents
  who are distraught at the possibility that their daughters and sons
  might marry someone from another "religious family."
- Other affiliation lines are **tenuous**; although people identify, they
  don't consciously place a great deal of importance on such ties.
  Yes, when surveyed they indicate that their preference is "Anglican," "Lutheran," or "Evangelical Free." But they might be open
  to trying another congregation that sounds interesting or is close
  by—especially if that congregation offers something special, say,
  for their kids.

- Still other affiliation lines have deteriorated to a fragile thread. Affiliates may identify with a group or its tradition, but want nothing more to do with it. They may have had their "fill" of religion, perhaps have been close to abuse and scandal, or simply feel that they have "graduated" from "that kind of religion." Here the affiliation lines are **tattered**.

- And some lines are **tangled**. Religious identification, as we all know, is sometimes less than perfectly clear. Mothers and fathers may not have identified with the same group, a person may have had involvement with a variety of groups, religious intermarriage may be contributing to identification confusion.

Oh, what a tangled web we weave!

Sophia, who was Catholic, and her husband Michael, who was Jewish, weren't terribly interested in religion so they didn't need to make any decisions about what religion they would bring their baby up in. When Tiffany was old enough, she could decide for herself. But Sophie had an almost instinctive feeling that Tiffany must be baptized. When she mentioned that she had made an appointment with a priest to discuss baptism, Michael was shocked. While he wouldn't insist that Tiffany be brought up as a Jew, baptizing her felt like a public declaration that they were bringing her up as a Catholic.

—*Diane Forrest, "Mixed Marriage and Remarriage,"*
When a Couple Marries, *Wood Lake Books, 1991:8*

And then there are enormous variations in "the content behind the label." For example, about the only thing that an active Anglican and an inactive Anglican may have in common is the name, "Anglican." The same could be said for the involved and non-involved in pretty much any group. Commonality of name may be just about all people have in common.

That might, however, be enough. The fact that two people both view themselves as "Anglican" means that they do have something in common—some basic affinity—that may make it possible for them at least to have a conversation. An Anglican priest who makes a house call to a non-attending person who thinks of herself as an Anglican will have a far better chance of getting an initial hearing than, say, a door-knocking Baptist, Jehovah's Witness, or Hare Krishna.

Needless to say, the number of affiliates who were uncovered in the latest census readily exceeds the number of people who are found on church rolls. The ratios are approximately:

- 5 to 1 for Presbyterians,
- 3 to 1 for the United Church, Anglicans, Lutherans, and Baptists,
- around 2 to 1 for Pentecostals, Reformed, Alliance, and Mormons.

Affiliate pools by age
Actual numbers (in 1000's)

| | Total | Age group | | | | |
		<15	15–24	25–44	45–64	65+
National	26,994	5,689	3,833	9,194	5,386	2,932
Roman Catholic						
Outside Quebec	6,342	1,413	982	2,185	1,203	559
Inside Quebec	5,861	1,162	792	2,038	1,263	607
Mainline Protestants						
United	3,093	579	369	975	686	484
Anglican	2,188	373	276	692	494	353
Presbyterian	636	101	73	194	151	118
Lutheran	636	109	75	191	161	101
Conservative Protestants						
Baptist	663	135	93	212	133	91
Pentecostal	436	116	73	144	72	32
Mennonite	208	56	33	62	36	21
Reformed	119	35	19	34	21	10
Salvation Army	112	23	18	36	22	13
Alliance	59	17	8	20	10	4
Adventist	52	12	8	17	10	6
Other faiths						
Jewish	318	62	37	97	63	59
Islam	253	72	40	99	35	8
Jehovah's Witnesses	168	43	24	55	30	17
Buddhist	163	31	26	64	29	14
Hindu	157	38	24	62	26	6
Sikh	147	43	23	52	22	8
Latter Day Saints	101	31	16	30	16	8

Source: Computed from 1991 Census, Statistics Canada, Catalogue 93-319. Not all groups included .

To "think affiliate" is to understand which Canadians a group has the best chance of relating to.

That's not to suggest that a given church should refrain from trying to connect with other groups' inactive affiliates. Some readers will object that, "If people are not being ministered to by other groups, they are people we should be pursuing, regardless of their religious identities."

In theory, there is nothing wrong with such an outlook. Better that some group makes contact than no group at all.

My point, however, is this: **generally speaking, one's identification group has the best chance of making an initial contact.** In calling groups to "think affiliate," **I am not telling people where to stop, but where to start**.

A quick observation about immigrants. New arrivals to Canada have no history of religious affiliation here—but churches can pick up the lines of affinity that already exist for them. According to 1991 *Statistics Canada* data, roughly one in three people from Asian countries **arrived in Canada as Christians**, one in three identified with other world faiths, and the remaining third said they had no religious preference. The increasing number of arrivals from Latin American countries are overwhelmingly Roman Catholic. Surely it's a logical strategy for Canadian churches to be more diligent in pursuing these existing affiliations.

Affiliation lines run from churches to Canadians. It's like finding that there are telephone lines already connected to our homes or cottages—they just haven't been turned on. The lines of affiliation are in place; they simply need to be activated.

It is critically important for religious groups to recognize and accept the fact that **close to 90% of Canadians "think" that they are part of religious groups and their traditions.**

"Thinking affiliate" is the first step churches need to take in trying to connect with Canadians.

2 Think "Concentric"

The old tendency has been for religious groups, especially Protestants, to "think dichotomous"—in terms of "insiders" and "outsiders." Active affiliates are embraced and valued; less-active affiliates are essentially viewed as "drop-outs." In today's terms, such thinking would mean that about 5 million affiliates are on the inside, while some 15 million adult affiliates are on the outside.

Polarization is common in our culture today. Our cultural mindset tends to see everything as black or white, good or bad, in or out. We don't like dealing with shades of gray. This mindset is not very helpful in making collective life possible.

Likewise, the "dichotomous" mindset has not been especially productive for either ministry or member recruitment. A new model is required, and is readily available. This second important piece of the connection and ministry puzzle is learning to "think concentric."

Having "laid claim" to their affiliates, groups need to stop simply splitting them into actives and drop-outs. **Affiliates need to be viewed as people who are part of a group's pool, yet who are characterized by differing levels of involvement.**

Those involvement variations can be conceptualized as a series of concentric circles, starting with high participation and moving outward through modest involvement to little or no involvement.

While actual participation criteria for such "sorting" are somewhat arbitrary, I've suggested in *Unknown Gods* that it might be helpful to identify five categories of affiliates:

1. A core of close to 25% of the Canadians identify with the nation's religious groups and are highly involved, attending services on almost a weekly basis. They might be referred to as **active affiliates**.
2. Approximately another 25% are what we might call **marginal affiliates**. They identify with religious groups and appear in the churches anywhere between a few times a month to a few times a year.
3. Almost an additional 40% are what we could label **inactive affiliates**. They identify, but attend services only about once a year or less.
4. Some 10% of Canadians claim no religious affiliation. But, as we have seen, caution needs to be used in treating their placement in this category as permanent. About 8 in 10 "nones" are what might be termed **disaffiliates**, in that their parents do identify with a re-

ligious group; some 93% of these disaffiliates attend services less than once a year.

5. The remaining 2 in 10 of the "nones" (2% of all Canadians) could be categorized as **non-affiliates**—people who say they have no affiliation and were raised in homes where both parents also were "nones"; 96% say they attend services less than once a year.

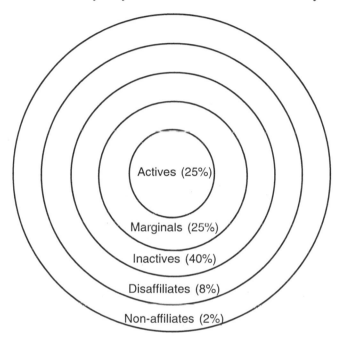

Actives (25%)

Marginals (25%)

Inactives (40%)

Disaffiliates (8%)

Non-affiliates (2%)

Let's be perfectly clear what this exercise is all about: **I am not categorizing just for the sake of categorizing.** What I am trying to do is

1. recognize that bona fide religious affiliates are out there in the Canadian population, and
2. recognize that they are not all the same "distance" from churches. The latter point is particularly important because of the implications for how churches might approach such people.
   - How they approach marginal affiliates who have sporadic involvement, for example, is one thing.
   - How they approach inactive affiliates, some of whom have little apparent interest, others of whom are downright antagonistic, is quite another.

Groups have to know what kinds of affiliates they are dealing with.

In thinking concentric, it's important for churches to recognize that the proportions of affiliates in the various categories differ from group to group and, in turn, sometimes from region to region. For example, nationally, the following variations in the proportion of "actives," "marginals," and "inactives" exist:[26]

- **Roman Catholics** tend to follow a "one-third, one-third, one-third" pattern; outside of Quebec, the proportion of actives is slightly higher and inactives somewhat lower than in Quebec.
- **Mainline Protestants** have roughly a "20-30-50" pattern, with little difference between Anglicans, the United Church, Lutherans, and Presbyterians.
- **Conservative Protestants** are almost the reverse, at around "50-20-30", with various evangelical groups—not identified explicitly by Statistics Canada—tending to fare a bit better than Baptists specifically.

Affiliate Pools of Select Canadian Groups
%'s rounded to nearest five points for simplicity

	Active	Marginal	Inactive	Totals
National	30	30	40	100
Roman Catholic				
Outside Quebec	35	35	30	100
In Quebec	25	35	40	100
Mainline Protestant				
United Church	15	35	50	100
Anglican	15	30	55	100
Presbyterian	20	30	50	100
Lutheran	20	35	45	100
Conservative Protestant				
Baptist	45	25	30	100
Others	55	15	30	100
Other World Faiths				
Eastern Orthodox	10	60	30	100
Jewish	25	40	35	100
Other	35	30	35	100

Source: Calculated from Bibby, Unknown Gods, *1993:172.*

- **Other World Faiths** differ with respect to their proportions of active and marginal affiliates, but tend to have about 35% in the inactive category.

The sobering element in such an analysis is the finding that such **large proportions of affiliates—30% or more—exist in every religious group.** That signals an awful lot of people with whom churches have an opportunity to engage in ministry—before they even think of looking to other groups' affiliates.

For those who nonetheless dream of ministering to entire cities and provinces and countries, I would offer this advice: continue both to "think affiliate" and "think concentric." Start at home and move outward. After you have "gone through your own," by all means consider moving on to other uninvolved affiliates who

A model for Presbyterian ministry

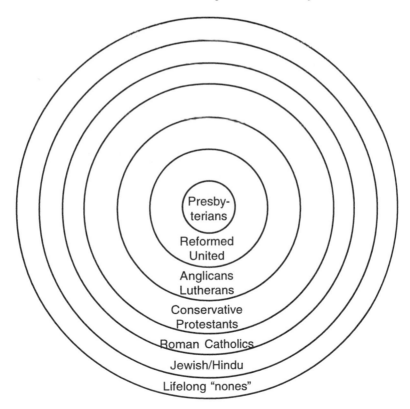

Presby-
terians

Reformed
United
Anglicans
Lutherans
Conservative
Protestants
Roman Catholics
Jewish/Hindu
Lifelong "nones"

are in need of ministry, beginning with those with whom you have the greatest affinity.

Presbyterians, for example, should start with people who think they are Presbyterians, and—if they wish to be enterprising—move on to "their cousins": uninvolved people with United or Christian Reformed ties, then to Anglicans and Lutherans, through a range of Conservative Protestant inactives, through lapsed Roman Catholics, eventually extending themselves further out to inactive people who are Jewish, Hindu, and the like, dealing finally with what may be the toughest of all categories—the lifelong "nones."

Lutherans, similarly, should start with those who think of themselves historically as Lutherans, moving out to their liturgical relatives in the Anglican and perhaps the Roman Catholic and Orthodox churches, then to others in the mainline Protestant churches of the Reformation, and so on.

Likewise, other groups should start at home and move outward, working first with the affiliates with whom they potentially have the greatest affinity.

For scoffers who think such a procedure too restrictive or mechanical, I would be audacious enough to point out that the strategy that I am proposing is simply a modern-day application of "the New Testament way." Faith was **first** shared with relatives and friends who were Jewish, **next** with Jewish strangers, and **then** with Gentiles. In keeping with such expansion, outreach started in Jerusalem, moved through Judea, to all of Palestine, to nearby Roman cities, and eventually reached Rome and then beyond.

"Thinking concentric" enables groups to recognize the diverse nature of their affiliates. It also enables them to understand with greater clarity some of the difficulties that are inherent in becoming adventurous and attempting to recruit the uninvolved who identify with other groups.

Concentric thinking puts groups in touch with those Canadians they are most likely to influence. Once such religious "kin folk" are identified, it's possible to move on to the important next stage of making contact.

3 Think "Relational"

The third piece of the connection and ministry puzzle is specifying the key link to concentrically-aligned affiliates: relationships.

By now it should be pretty clear that the image of the isolated individual who finds God or a church on his or her own is a figment of imagination. **The dominant sources of religious commitment and involvement are relational.**

- Individuals are introduced to God by other people.
- Individuals are introduced to churches by other people.

Social links are key both to the ideas people come to hold and to the organizations to which they belong. Basic social psychology tells us that ideas are socially instilled and socially sustained; similarly, basic sociology tells us that people are introduced to groups by other people.[27] Without social links, there are no ideas and there is no group involvement.

What is true of ideas and group life generally is true for religion specifically. Social sources are indispensable to religious commitment and religious involvement.

Religious groups that are serious about connecting with Canadians and responding to their spiritual, personal, and social needs will ensure that social links are a deliberate and conscious part of their ministries.

One of the largest and best known churches in the United States is Bill Hybels' Willow Creek Community Church, outside Chicago. Started in 1975, it has a weekly attendance of some 15,000. The church has received considerable attention, both because of its growth and because of its innovative ministry efforts aimed at Baby Boomers. Yet Hybels himself points out that his weekend "seeker services" won't accomplish anything "unless Christians build credible relationships" with people outside the church, and "invite them to church and talk to them about their faith."[28]

The findings are simply decisive: religious groups "grow their own" through members sharing faith with their children, assisted by church programs such as Sunday schools and youth activities. "Farm systems" have to be in place if faith is to be transmitted and groups are to remain viable.

- "Social bridges" into religious groups come in the form of friends and family members.
- "Social networks" develop as people live their everyday lives in relationships. They are members of families, have circles of friends, have a variety of acquaintances.

A minister tries another church

I am a preacher. Last summer, I decided to try a church quite different from my own. I decided to go to a nearby "Bible Church" that has been experiencing impressive growth.

As the worship hour drew nearer, I found my anxiety level rising. The dog could use some exercise. The lawn needed mowing. The gardens needed weeding. I have always wondered what's on television on a Sunday morning.

Church wasn't a particularly inviting thought. Only because I was determined to carry out "the experiment" did I persist. It would have been easier to go with my neighbor—she's a regular attender—but, as luck would have it, there was no sign of her. So I went by myself.

As I drove into the parking lot, my anxiety level rose even higher! I didn't know what was expected of me or what they actually do. As I entered the building, I actually found myself perspiring. I was greeted at the door by the person on duty. We said good morning and shook hands. I followed some people up the stairs, hoping that they knew where they were going—and that it was the same place I wanted to go. I sat at the back.

As the service progressed, I began to relax somewhat. After it was over, I realized that it actually hadn't been all that bad—in fact, I rather enjoyed it. I was able to remain anonymous and slipped out quickly after the service.

The experience gave me a whole new appreciation for what people who don't attend church much must go through on a Sunday morning. It's pretty tough to do it alone. Who needs all that anxiety on the day of rest?

—*Robin Wilkie, Minister, Waterdown United Church, Ontario*

Efforts to relate to uninvolved affiliates need to see them as **people who are part of social groupings**, rather than as isolated individuals.

- Programs aimed at children and teenagers, for example, need to be sensitive to the role that friends play in their lives. As my friend and colleague Don Posterski pointed out in our book, *Teen Trends,* young people are not so much inclined to ask, "What's taking place?" as they are to ask, "Who's going to be there?"

● Groups cannot, however, aim efforts at young people, without also taking into account their connection to parents—any more than groups would target parents without recognizing their connection to their children. Ministry must be aimed at friendship clusters and entire families.

Attempts to relate to affiliates have to be sensitive to their social environments.

Those efforts also require superb record-keeping. As people who constitute "concentric circles of involvement" are located, data bases need to be generated that include pertinent demographic and social characteristics. I'll go into more detail on this in Chapters 4 and 5.

Fortunately, the timing for such charting of affiliates couldn't be better. **Religious groups today are in a better position than any groups in history to obtain, store, and update information on their affiliates.** Technology, through such contributions as the computer and the fax machine, has provided religious groups with unprecedented data analysis capabilities and communication possibilities. Well-equipped "saints" need to embrace and make good use of these timely and valuable gifts.

Soft touch and hard data can represent powerful allies in relating to affiliates.

4 Think "Balance"

So far I have identified three pieces of the connection-ministry puzzle:

1. start with affiliates,
2. view them as being varying distances from the church,
3. recognize that the key links to them will be relational.

A critically important fourth piece consists of what the church has to bring—its "product." Here the key is "thinking balance"—responding to spiritual, personal, and social needs with ministry that gives balanced emphasis on God, self, and society.

As we have seen, the research tells us that most Canadians are not looking for churches—or even religion, at least as many of them understand it. But people do express spiritual and supernatural interest, have personal desires and needs, and want to experience enhanced interpersonal life. Therein, I have been maintaining, lies religion's great challenge and opportunity.

A religion that begins with God and that proceeds to minister to the spiritual, personal, and social needs of Canadians is a religion that has the potential to have a profound impact on Canadians.

- It is far more powerful than secular competitors that focus primarily on self or society, in that it brings the resources of God to bear on both.
- It integrates the central dimensions of our existence—the spiritual, the personal, and the social.

Tragically, as I have pointed out in *Fragmented Gods,* religious groups have often had considerable difficulty putting these three themes together.

- Some groups have stressed God and salvation, while playing down self and society.
- Other groups have emphasized self, and have minimized the importance of God and society.
- Still others have focused on society, and neglected both God and self.

Nevertheless, in light of the nature of faith and the needs at hand, the three themes have to be fused. My plea to religious groups is the same as it was in 1987:

> *The gods are currently fragmented. They lie dismantled, in pieces. But the recognition of religion's poverty can lead to the rediscovery of its potential. Reconnection is not beyond the realm of possibility.*[29]

Groups that set out to address, in integrated fashion, the spiritual, individual, and social needs of Canadians will find people to be responsive. Not everyone—but far more than the 20% or so who currently are being drawn to the churches. Why? Because that kind of faith is in touch with Canadian desires and needs.

And the beauty of "the fit"? It doesn't involve catering to consumers and sacrificing integrity. On the contrary. In presenting an integrated ministry emphasizing God, self, and society, churches have the opportunity to epitomize integrity.

Religious groups that start with God, and proceed to embrace self and society, have something powerful to bring to Canadians. Balance between the three themes, however, is essential.

5 Think "Collective"

The connection and ministry puzzle is still missing one extremely important piece. Because the vast majority of Canadians continue to identify with one religious group or another, by now it should be fairly clear that no one group is going to be able to do it all. What needs to be done can be done. But it will have to be done together.

- It's not a question of good intentions.
- It's not a question of solid ministry.
- It's not a question of human resources.
- It's not even a question of dollars.

The issue is one of access. **Because of the fact that Canadians are so reluctant to abandon "the religious families" of their childhoods, even the most enterprising and resourceful efforts of one group have built-in limits.**

- Roman Catholics run up against walls when they attempt to relate to Protestants.
- Mainline Protestants find that recruitment is tough when they direct their energies at Conservative Protestants and Jews.
- Conservative Protestants know by now that evangelistic efforts among Catholics, Hindus, and lifelong "nothings" have not exactly met with resounding success.

Even within denominations, individual congregations find themselves facing limits as they deal with "their own" affiliates. For example, a person who is contacted may

- prefer a more liberal or conservative religious style within the same denomination;
- be more "at home" with another congregation in the same denomination that has quite different social characteristics;
- turn out to be hostile toward the group with which he or she formally identifies.

It's very clear from the research that **the affiliational diversity of Canadians, combined with their personal preferences, make it impossible for any one congregation or national group to do it all.**

"Lone ranger" efforts are nothing less than foolish expeditions—not to mention masochistic exercises in bad stewardship—demonstrating apparent obliviousness to some rather reliable advice offered some 2000 years ago about wasting a lot of valuable seed on a lot of questionable rocks.

Yet, here again, something that at first may seem to be a negative for the churches, on further examination, emerges as potentially an enormous plus. No one group can do it all. **But if they will choose to work together, Canada's religious groups can have an enormous impact on Canadian lives.**

If they are willing to "think collective," they can

- readily locate each other's affiliates,
- share insights on how to relate to them, and
- help each other to engage in the kind of balanced ministries that are so urgently required.

A quick parable. A Baptist church thought it would be a good idea to let the community know that they existed, and set out to hang information paks on 10,000 doorknobs. But, in glancing over a *Stats Canada* breakdown on the community's demographics, the senior pastor realized that at least 5,000 of those doorknobs were attached to Roman Catholic homes. (Such urban breakdowns are available in one Statistics Canada census volume, catalog number 93-319. In smaller communities, it might be possible to get a rough sense of ethnic/denominational proportions simply from scanning the telephone book; eastern European and Latin American names, for example, are likely to be predominantly Roman Catholic.)

In fact, this pastor wasn't all that excited about Catholicism. But he was a realist. So he drove over to St. Patrick's and had a chat with the local priest. The upshot was that they agreed to put together a packet that invited people to share in the services and programs of the Baptist Church if they were Protestant, and St. Pat's if they were Catholic. Each church eventually distributed 5,000 packets each. It was a start in the direction of collective ministry.

Unfortunately, this was just a parable I made up. It didn't happen.

But it could happen and it must happen. Meeting needs, particularly of a personal and social nature, is extremely difficult for one congregation or one denomination to achieve. A wide range of services and programs is required. It necessitates **cooperative, collective ministry.**

There's another important sociologically-grounded reason why churches have to "think collective." **If religious groups are to contribute to the changing of lives, they have to be in a position to influence the environments in which people live.** That means that they must be able to have an impact on social structures, including key institutions such as government and media.

Social change of that magnitude calls for the collective effort of religious groups in communities, cities, provinces, and nation. Otherwise, it will never happen! Institutions can ignore one or two groups; they can't ignore a majority of them.

In collective ministry, diversity acually works to the benefit of the churches. In a very real way, collective ministry is driven by necessity. Everyone has limited access—not to mention limited resources. Yet, the limitations of individual groups can be converted into considerable collective strength. **The diverse needs of the population can only be met by a diverse Church.**

The good news is that those diverse needs **can** be met by a diverse Church. If Canada's churches choose to work together, much can be accomplished.

It may sound audacious to say it, but—as my mother used to tell me—sometimes if you don't say something it never is said. The puzzle—the question of how declining churches can connect with and respond to Canadians who are in need of ministry—is no longer a mystery. It has been solved by the research.

- Canadians continue to identify with religious traditions, providing invaluable "connection lines" to the groups.
- People are still "out there," comprising affiliate pools; but they often are not associating their needs with what the churches have to offer.

- Affiliates can fairly easily be found, with the key links to the groups being relational and techological.
- Their spiritual, personal, and social needs, however, all have to be explicitly addressed by the churches; they can be, with integrity.
- The key to a concerted response to the needs of Canadians is the collective and complementary ministry of a wide range of religious groups and individual congregations.

It's all remarkably straightforward. To the chagrin of the gods, however, that doesn't mean that what needs to happen will necessarily happen.

"Herod was greatly puzzled,
yet he liked to listen to him."
—Mark 6:20

Chapter 3

Making sure that something happens

Having looked at the key findings and crucial implications, let's take a quick breather—and ask ourselves what happens next.

You see, in presenting ideas across the country in the last decade or so, I have found that up to this point, audiences typically are interested, reasonably receptive, and even a shade enthused. Of course the reaction is mixed—there are some people who feel overwhelmed by "the stats," others who come alive with the implications, and a few who never really quite see the relationship between the findings and the implications.

Still, overall, people tend to be pleasant, tell me they found the material interesting, and encourage me to keep up the good work.

Unfortunately, after everyone leaves, I'm not sure that anything really happens. In the past, when I saw my role as primarily the sociologist who should provide people with clearer perception, I was content to leave "the rest" up to the groups. If something happened, good; if not—well, at least I had done my part as best I felt I could.

Maybe it's a sign of age; I prefer to think of it rather as a sign of passion and excitement. But these days, **I believe that it is critically important that Canada's religious groups seize the tremendous opportunity at hand—because Canadians need what they are capable of bringing.**

Things need to happen. Yet anyone familiar with social change generally—and institutional change specifically—knows well that

---

I am indebted to "Bud" Phillips for reflections that have contributed to this chapter.

just because something **should** happen doesn't mean that it **will** happen.

So before we move on and talk about some tangible ways in which religious groups might respond to the current situation, let's take a few pages to reflect on some of the reasons why nothing **may** happen, in order to ensure that in some groups and some congregations, something **will** happen.[30]

Differing views of mission

People involved in religious groups at the denominational and local levels have strong feelings about what the church is for, its purpose or mission. These feelings will color their perception of what I have been talking about. **Not everyone hears the research news the same way.** For example,

- some view the church's primary role as **evangelist**, and hear that a great opportunity to reach unchurched Canadians for Christ;
- some view the church's primary role as **prophet**, and hear that fewer are willing to succumb to the demands of the gospel;
- some view the church's primary role as **church builder**, and hear great opportunity to experience greater church growth;
- some view the church's primary role as **nurturer**, and hear that fewer people are choosing to have their spiritual and personal needs met by the church;
- some view the church's primary role as **servant**, and hear that there is a great opportunity to minister to the personal and social needs of larger numbers of Canadians.

Diverse interpretations of the times are in turn accompanied by very different emotional responses.

- Those who believe in the opportunity to **evangelize**, and those who see the possibility of great **church growth**, tend to be upbeat and enthused.
- Those who believe in the opportunity to **minister** also are inclined to be positive—tempered by the realization that unlimited opportunities to minister are not matched by unlimited resources.
- Those who believe in being **prophetic** are frequently characterized by a mood of somber conviction and unwavering determination—faithfulness must be upheld, regardless of the costs.

● Those who focus on **nurture** tend to have something of a fatalistic attitude toward the declining numbers. If the resources of their denominations and congregations translate into financial viability, some adopt an attitude of being in transition, a "ministry in the meantime." If, however, finances are a threat to survival, the mood predictably shifts to concern, even to immobilizing despair. As one minister told me this past summer, "Our treasurer says that our church has six months to live. It doesn't exactly put us in a ministry mode."

The news that the sociologist brings obviously may go no further than initially being heard by diverse ears; that in itself, incidentally, is no small achievement! It seems to me, however, that the **research and implication news is not applicable to one camp over another**—despite the tendency of some who to want to dismiss my research as irrelevant to them because of my sociology, ideology, ecclesiology, theology, and yes, even my biography!

The facts are there for evaluation and verification:
● Canadians are in need of ministry.
● The churches are capable of responding.

This is not a time for defense, not a time to huddle together and accept or bemoan the era in which we just happen to live. It rather is a time for offense, a time for the churches to do everything they can to reach out and minister to Canadians. This is a time for evangelism and growth, and also a time for service; a time to take tough prophetic stands and also a time to comfort and nurture.

Whether one's dominant view of mission is evangelism, church growth, service, prophecy, or nurture doesn't matter: ministry—diversely conceptualized—needs to be taking place. Larger numbers of Canadians need to be touched by the churches, because larger numbers of Canadians than ever before are expressing spiritual, personal, and social needs.

Lack of leadership

If Canada's churches are to be mobilized to connect with Canadians, **leaders must catch the vision and help to bring it about.** Without the support and stimulus of leaders, little will happen.

Leaders who are committed to acting on the research and its implications face at least four centrally important tasks:

Education
Other leaders, both clergy and laity, need to be similarly informed of the opportunity and need that exists in the 1990s. They also require considerable assistance in developing ministries and strategies for relating to larger numbers of Canadians. The major sources of such support conceivably will include denominations and theological colleges, including continuing education in the form of courses and workshops. Strong, individual congregations might also take the lead. Better research, management, and computer skills are essential.

Policy
Policies pertaining to identifying and ministering to the large pools of affiliates need to be adopted denominationally and congregationally, so that clarity exists with respect to the goals and means of dealing with affiliates.

Strategies
Strategies grounded in available information and specific congregational circumstances must be developed, disseminated, and utilized, with denominations playing a leadership, consultative role in relating to their member congregations.

Initiatives
Initiatives have to be handled with care. What is proposed is sometimes less important than who proposes it. If churches are to engage in greater ministry to Canadians, sensitivity has to be used in determining whether the call for change should be initiated at the national level, for example, the local level or—perhaps ideally—simultaneously from both.

Discussions with people across the country make it very clear that, as leaders relate to each other and to rank and file church members, **two key factors affecting receptivity are confidence and trust.** In conveying to denominations and congregations the importance of churches being better connected to Canadians, leaders have to be able to combine passion and conviction with clarity about what the proposal is all about and why it is so necessary. It's been said before, but it needs to be said again: what's required is more than facilitation and coordination; **leaders must lead.**

People who lead with a clear sense of what needs to happen and an openness to the collective insights of others as to how it will happen will contribute much to the realization of connection and ministry.

On receptivity to change

"What are you looking for in a new minister?" As interim moderator of a congregation in Vancouver, I asked this question of the session. "What are your hopes and dreams? What kind of gifts are needed by the person you call?" Several elders responded, and the last to speak did so softly, but firmly. "I have one burning desire, and that is to come into the sanctuary each week and be challenged to change." That elder was 90 years old, and he understood.

Church leaders do well to reread regularly Jesus' farewell discourses in John's Gospel (chapters 13-17). Christ promised the Holy Spirit's presence, and in the following months and years the Advocate prodded, challenged, and confronted the apostles to make the changes necessary to bring the church to a more vigorous witness to the Gospel.

Teachability is the mark of reforming courage. It takes patience to learn. It takes determination to change. When comfortable habits are—uncomfortably—broken, faithful participants in Christ's mission are able to take greater risks for the Gospel.

—*Brian J. Fraser, Dean, St. Andrew's Hall,*
Vancouver School of Theology.[31]

Missing motivation

And now for the tough question: "Why should we?" Or, put more cynically, "Why bother?"

For all the debate about motivation, there seem to be two main reasons why we are moved to do what we do: **self-interest** and **interest in others,** egoism and altruism. While some philosophers and psychiatrists might limit motives only to the former, I, for one, think that people occasionally, if somewhat rarely, act out of concern for other people.[32]

If churches are going to make an effort to connect with Canadians, they are going to have to be motivated. Leaders and members have to believe that it is in their best interests and the best interests of Canadians for churches to go to the trouble of getting in contact with their affiliates and proceeding to attempt to engage in ministry.

After all, there are some religious groups and congregations who are reasonably content with things, just as they are. Change would mean adjustment—new goals, new activities, and, if all goes well, an infusion of new people into church life. That's all pretty scary. Behind closed doors and fairly closed minds, people can be expected to murmur, "Can't we just keep on ministering, and avoid all that change stuff? Is it really worth all the trouble?"

Appeals to leaders and from leaders will have to be both egoistic and altruistic.

- On the **self-interest** side, to be willing to change, leaders and members will have to believe that meaningful ministry is taking place. One of the spin-offs of effective ministry will be growing congregations, more members, and greater human and financial resources with which to enhance ministry. Canadians who find their lives enriched by the churches will be willing to give time and money to the churches.

- On the **interest of others** side, to be willing to change, leaders and members will have to believe that people who need ministry are receiving it. Although they may not be showing up in churches, nonetheless they are having spiritual, personal, and social needs met.

New members, anyone?

Often churches will say, "We want to grow," but really don't mean it. Acceptance of newcomers into the life and ministry of a church often carries a price that the old-timers are unwilling to pay. It means they would have to give up some power, share some of the minister's time and energy with others, and adjust to change. It means they would have to deal with not knowing "who all those people are." (After all, "stranger" means danger in a small community, and newer people almost always are seen as a threat.)

—*Perry Bell, writing in* Congregations, *published by the Alban Institute, Sept.-Oct., 1994:10.*

If members and leaders cannot be convinced that efforts to extend ministry to larger numbers of Canadians is worthwhile for them and/or for others, things will continue on pretty much as they are now. The opportunity for ministry awaiting Canada's religious groups will go largely unrealized.

On the other hand, the opportunity of touching more Canadians with Christian faith is an attainable dream, which has the potential—I believe—to motivate a good many people. They need to be given the chance to embrace and endorse such a possibility.

Shortage of resources

Let's not kid ourselves. One of the main reasons why people will be reluctant to get excited about reaching out and ministering to Canadians is the cost. As a minister of a large Baptist church in western Canada told me bluntly, "Focusing on uninvolved affiliates is fine. But I have to juggle it with other important priorities that also require money and personnel. There's only so many dollars and hours to go around."

- Active members need to be looked after.
- Existing programs and activities compete for scarce resources.
- Fixed costs have to be met.

Such concerns are both real and legitimate. Consequently, ministry to uninvolved affiliates has to find its place on the resource priority lists of denominations and congregations. Costs and benefits have to be carefully weighed. Leaders and members have to be convinced that connecting with uninvolved affiliates warrants premier attention.

Some groups and congregations can be expected to be reluctant to take such resource chances, questioning whether focusing on affiliates is what amounts to "a good investment" in either growing churches or meaningful ministry.

The real question, however, is whether Canadians outside the churches are to be reached, or not. If they are, some groups are going to have to take some chances with time and money—at least to engage in some pilot project efforts. Otherwise, that gap between the churches and people is not going to be bridged. Far too many people across Canada will continue to go hungry.

The rigidity of congregational culture

As we all know, congregations, like other social groups, have their own distinct cultures—just as people have different personalities.

- They have their own distinctive demographic and social characteristics.
- They have their individual histories and identities, their own views as to why they exist and what they want to accomplish.
- They have different styles, levels of energy, and resource bases.
- They vary in both their receptivity to change and in their ability to change.

For all these reasons, **congregations can be expected to respond very differently—and individualistically—to the call to connect with Canadians.** Some can be expected to respond readily; others will not; still others may feel that they cannot.

Given the reality of congregational cultures, combined with the prevalent value placed on local autonomy, whole denominations undoubtedly will be slow to respond to what I am calling for.

But **the turnaround needs to start somewhere.** I can't think of a more realistic place than single congregations and local ministerials. There is no reason why individual congregations in certain locales that "catch the connection and ministry vision" cannot—with or without denominational support—"pilot" the effort to make contact with affiliates. In the process, they will be able to demonstrate to other congregations and groups the importance of engaging in collective ministry to affiliates.

A time to look... and a time to leap

It's hard to get people to look at old things in new ways. It's even harder to get people to move from just looking to actually leaping, expecting good things to follow. Even Simon Peter, you may recall, came bounding out of the boat to walk on water. But the biblical story tells us that he had limited faith in the success of the exercise, and just about drowned.

In life, timing is everything. The religious situation in Canada today represents a remarkable opportunity for religious groups.

Because of the legacy of Christianity and other religions in this country, the majority of the populace continue to identify with groups, possess religious memory, are receptive to spirituality, and exhibit personal and social needs that are consistent with the God, self, and society themes so central to faith.

The identification lines are still in place, and the need for ministry is extensive. No one knows for sure how long the current identification situation will exist. Without some kind of church involvement, maybe 20 years, maybe 50. But in lieu of church ties, the coming reality is inevitable. Religious identification and memory will fade.

When that happens, **the current identification lines to religious groups will gradually dissipate. At that point, a remarkable opportunity will disappear.**

This unique "window in time" must not be ignored. Now is the time for groups to act, to follow the lines of affiliation and affinity that connect them with Canadians, and attempt to put people in touch with faith's spiritual, personal, and relational themes.

For those individuals and groups that wish to respond, tangible strategies are readily available.

Okay, so what's next?

I belong to one of the many declining churches that William Easum talks about. Recently, I attended a workshop on the Easum approach. Frankly, I found the analysis of present woes more convincing than the remedies. The question of where you start with a traditional congregation was not effectively answered.

You say we need to identify our non-church-going target. The question is how? I suspect that (a) most of those people out there have little idea of what goes on in a church, and (b) most of them have very transient notions of their actual needs.

Where do we go from here?

—*A lay leader looking for help, in a letter of December, 1994.*

---

*"Let the children come to me,
for the kingdom of heaven belongs
to such as these."*—Matthew 19:14

Chapter 4
Creating and retaining affiliates

Let's begin talking tangibles by reminding everyone where the connecting has to start.

A simple knock on the door tells the story. "Hello, we have a magazine we think you might be interested in..." You look down and see the word *Watchtower*. Unless you are among the 1% of Canadians who view themselves as Jehovah's Witnesses, you're probably not exactly thrilled by the visit.

But let's not just pick on the "JW's." Over the course of your life, ask yourself how excited you would be to answer that front door and find someone on the doorstep who introduced himself or herself as an "Anglican," a "Baptist," "Christian Reformed," "United Church," "Mormon," "Roman Catholic," and so on.

Invariably, your response depended on "the religious distance" involved—how close or how far the door-knocker was from your own identification group.

Which should tell you a great deal about where to start and where not to start when you look at that map of the nation or province or city or community. **The logical place to begin is with affinity lines.** In Canada, those lines are already in place, connecting churches and their affiliates.

What is needed is for churches to take those identification lines seriously. Churches that are serious about connecting with Canadians will begin by **thinking affiliate.**

Outside of the churches, such a procedure is taken for granted. It is referred to as "targeting." Successful interest groups and manufacturers don't go after everybody. On the contrary, they know very well that they have to **target** those segments of the population most likely to be interested in what they have to offer. Does anyone need to be told that feminist groups target women, that football ads target men, that hospital fundraisers target the affluent, that rock music videos target the young?

Not everyone is interested in what Roman Catholics have to offer. The same is true of Anglicans, Pentecostals, and so on. Trying to relate to the entire Canadian population—something religious groups invariably claim they are attempting to do—is more than simply intimidating; it is unproductive, poor marketing, and sometimes pretty bad stewardship.

A Korean evangelical Baptist pastor in Ontario tells the story of going to his board with "a great idea" about distributing videos to his neighborhood. They bought the idea and proceeded to distribute 2,000 videos at about $8 a crack—adding up to a cool $16,000. The church heard from **two** people. A few months later, he again approached the board, this time with a book distribution idea—about 2,000 books at $5 apiece, for an investment of around $10,000. This time they heard from **four** people.

Several months later, this pastor says that he once more came to the board. Fortunately, he was told bluntly, "Please—don't bring us any more ideas!"

In cold hard cash, the first two affiliates cost the church $8,000 each; the next four cost $2,500 each. Ethics aside, they could have more effectively **hired** people to come to church!

There's no need for such a waste of resources. Ongoing identification translates into great news for religious groups that want to relate to Canadians. **Churches already have affinity lines in place that are the absolute envy of other organizations that want to expand.** Religious name-brand loyalty is rampant. Thanks to family religious socialization, all but a very small percentage of Canadians already identify with the Roman Catholic, Mainline Protestant, Conservative Protestant, and Other Faith religious families of their parents.

The entire city, the entire country—and, for that matter, the entire world—can be seen as the ministry field of churches. Yet, the reality is that many Canadians are not having their spiritual, personal, and social needs met by any of the churches. That has to end!

The beginning of that end lies with groups recognizing that identification lines **are** in place. The connection cable has already been laid; what's required now is for religious groups to experiment with transmission.

Affiliates, of course, did not just suddenly appear. They were literally created over the generations by religious groups and their members. While considerable energy needs to be given to responding to them, it is also critically important to continue to create them—to be constantly adding to the affiliate pool. **That's where our discussion of strategies for healthy churches connecting with unchurched Canadians needs to start.**

Creating affiliates

On the surface, Sigmund Freud and the writer of Proverbs and Branch Rickey don't seem to have much in common.

- Freud, of course, is the much-maligned founder of psychoanalysis who thought that religion was something that got in the way of good minds and would one day soon be replaced by science.
- The writer of Proverbs was a conscientious and meticulous scribe who attempted—with assistance of others—to lay down the collective wisdom of the Hebrew people.
- Branch Rickey was the general manager of the old Brooklyn Dodgers, who is best known for introducing the first black player—Jackie Robinson—to major league baseball.

Yet they had a very important thought in common.

- Freud maintained that ideas are passed on through relationships, and that religion specifically is learned like anything else—like the alphabet or the multiplication table.[33]
- The writer of Proverbs admonished children to listen to what their parents have to say, and reminded parents that what they passed on to their children would essentially stick with them for life.[34]
- Rickey recognized that top-flight ball teams don't emerge out of nothing; players have to be developed over time, and he consequently began to assemble baseball's first farm system. Although—to the best of my knowledge—Rickey never said it, successful and effective religious groups also need to have farm systems in place.

The research is conclusive: **people who value religion are people who are exposed to religion through social contacts, primarily parents, friends, and partners.** Further, people who come to value participation in religious groups are primarily the offspring of members. Support for that assertion just keeps on coming.

My 1994 *Unitrends* analysis of people who are the most involved members of the United Church shows that about 80% came from United Church homes and attended services regularly as children. They are people who are involved today for one key reason: they see faith and the church as playing a significant role in their lives—something, in turn, that most began to experience when they were growing up.

The kind of ministries that are needed in Canada today require that churches be sound organizations. That means that they have to have a core of faithful members who not only benefit from the ministry of the churches, but also are capable and willing to provide the human and financial resources that are necessary in order for ministry to other affiliates to take place.

Such stability at the core requires churches to constantly create their own—to produce new affiliates. It's no exaggeration to say that **the numerical viability of religious groups depends primarily on their ability to retain members' children over their lifetimes.** And that's where Freud, the Proverbs writer, and Rickey all come in.

Canada's churches have to consciously transmit an appreciation for faith and ministry through relationships. Following Rickey, they need to make sure that they have solid **farm systems** in place. Otherwise, when the current roster ages and players retire, the team won't have the necessary replacements.

It therefore is essential that
1. programs and activities be established for children, teenagers, and young adults;
2. young people be fully integrated into congregational and denominational life as soon as is possible, in accordance with their ability to participate and contribute;
3. superb records be kept on these young affiliates, drawing on the

best available technology, so that they never get "lost"—even if they drift away from active participation for a period.

Developing farm systems

One of the most prevalent myths about churches is that numbers decrease primarily because people drop out. Listen carefully: "it just ain't so!"

The primary reason that numbers drop nationally is because groups are unable to replace members who die. Locally, they decline because they are not able to replace people who move, as well as pass away.

In looking at the American scene, Lyle Schaller notes that, between 1969 and 1993, United Methodists, for example, removed from their membership rolls nearly three million members who died. "Most of those members who died were not replaced," he writes, adding, "that is the biggest single reason why the membership... dropped by nearly 2.5 million during that quarter century."[35]

If denominations and congregations are to have viable futures, church schools, youth groups, and youth activities must be in place. Congregations that don't have Sunday schools or youth groups, yet think that things "go in cycles" and "eventually will work themselves out," are dreaming. Some might manage to remain numerically afloat by recruiting geographically—by luring transfers from other congregations within their denomination, something like attracting baseball "free agents." But such congregations will contribute few affiliates to their denominations and religious families.

And people who pin their hopes on miracles—such as "Baby Boomers" suddenly coming back to church—better think again. Yes, I'm familiar with those *Newsweek* and *Maclean's* stories about all those boomers heading back to church, with their kids in tow. It's a nice thought—enough to replace those grim looks on the faces of many church leaders with big smiles, faster heartbeats, and no little relief.

But as I pointed out in *Unknown Gods,* it's not happening, in Canada or—for that matter—in the U.S. For all the excitement, my research friends south of the border, such as Clark Roof and Dave Roozen, have been misunderstood.[36] They've been saying that **some** baby boomers are going back to church, but **most aren't.** We've been finding the same thing in Canada: **some** boomers are returning, but the majority are not. And the returnees are not showing up in sufficient numbers to offset losses through death and dropout.

There are no shortcuts to permanent numerical stability. Collectively-speaking, without "farm systems," the numbers simply won't be there in the future.

Similarly, we hear a lot about "church planting" these days, whereby numerical growth is seen as almost the inevitable result of starting new congregations. However, the procedure assumes that a nucleus of active affiliates already exists in the community. **True church planting begins with affiliate planting.**

The pool has to be present in order for congregations to be born. It all starts with children.

It's time to turn to Boomers' kids

All of this attention being given Baby Boomers is irrelevant to the question of what to do about the current attendance drop-off. The Boomers are a historical artifact—a horse already out of the barn. The future of the churches depends on the behavior and choices of Generation X, since the hoped-for "return to church" of the Boomers will provide only a short-term, 15 to 25 year relief. If we want to be helpful to the churches, we should be focusing on the next—not the previous—generation, no matter how unique and fascinating we might find Baby Boomers to be.

We need to accept that our time is passing, and that the important fertile ground for the future is the generation only now coming of age.

—note given to me by Peter Halvorson of the University of Connecticut, following a panel discussion on Baby Boomers in November, 1994. Printed with his permission.

I recognize that in some demographic instances, there may be virtually no children or teenagers to work with. So be it; that doesn't negate the feeder principle. The point is that churches which **do** have access to young people in their congregations and their communities need to make sure that they work with them, and work with them well.

Sometimes there is merit in sending out symbolic messages

about farm systems. Just recently, someone told me about having only one teen in their small rural church. So, in starting up a youth group, instead of calling it, "the Young People's Group," they called it, "Darrell's Group." The first time the group met, guess what? Darrell brought a friend and they were already up to two! That little church is helping to develop the denomination's "feeder system." It thereby is making an essential contribution.

As congregations attempt to minister to youth, the finding that "religion is relational" needs to be kept foremost in mind. **Children and teenagers must be seen as linked to friends and parents.**

- Church schools, for example, should ensure that settings are structured to enable friends to be together. The United Church almost lost one of its future moderators, when an overly officious Sunday school superintendent tried to force Anne Squire, as a child, into a class that was her age but two grades behind her in school.
- Program and activity opportunities need to exist that allow parents to participate both with and without their children.
- Teen groups have to be structured to maximize the possibility of friends being able to participate together—sometimes with parents present, often without them.

At the teen level, collective ministry is potentially an important plus. One church cannot do it all when it comes to young people. It's not only a case of limited resources; it's also a matter that friendships and dating commonly cross religious group boundaries, especially when some groups are not very large. There is no virtue in separating people who would like to be together, and then telling them to "have fun!" They may well choose to skip the activity altogether. One way to get teens together is to have groups work together.

Religious groups that attempt to share existing resources, as well as work together to develop innovative programs and activities, will have the best chance of keeping and attracting youth. Musical events, parties, retreats, camps, trips, and the like that are sponsored collectively will become more attractive and more enjoyable to young people—not to mention probably experiencing a numbers jump as well. In the process, young people will also be introduced to the idea of collective ministry, and will see some of its benefits first-hand.

Yes, you may lose "your" teenagers to the local Bible chapel if you work together with them; the alternative, though, is probably to lose those teenagers entirely.

Upgraded quality, greater quantity, collective effort—it doesn't sound all that bad.

Sustaining interest

It's one thing to create affiliates; it's another thing to keep them. The 1994 *Unitrends* national study of United Church members and leaders has come up with very similar findings about "dropouts" as those unveiled in the *Anglitrends* study of Toronto Anglicans a decade earlier.

- Considerable numbers of people who were raised in the church drop out during their late teens and early 20s.
- If they return at all, they begin re-emerging in their late 20s and especially their 30s, some in their early 40s.
- However, if they have not returned by around the age of 40, chances are pretty good that they are not coming back.

Yet I've argued for some time that there is nothing written in the stars that requires young people to drop out during their late teen years. I suspect that most who say goodbye to the churches do so for one main reason: they don't find churches to be particularly enjoyable or gratifying environments.[37]

These are years when young people are emerging into adulthood in a multidimensional way. They need direction, but they also need room to explore and grow, reflect and express themselves. My hunch is that they will be more than happy to be around people who can find that direction/room balance.

I'm not so sure that churches have been particularly adept at finding the combination. Our youth surveys, for example, find that when it comes to enjoyment

- Canadian teenagers think of friends and music, sports and television, pets and even parents, sometimes jobs and occasionally even school; but

- the last place most teens expect to find enjoyment is the church. Just 15% of 15- to 19-year-olds say they receive a high level of enjoyment from religious groups. Roman Catholic young people are slightly more negative than Protestants.

If young people are going to stay, then they have to be treated like the rest of us. They have to find that they are **respected, valued, wanted, and needed**. They have to find that the church environment is one that is in touch with their spiritual, personal, and relational needs—including their enjoyment of music!

Churches that are "old boys' clubs" and "old girls' clubs" will understandably not be places where teenagers and young adults will want to hang out.

In short, like everyone else, **young people have to find that church involvement is worth their time.** As part of being treated as full-fledged people, children and teens need to be seen as an important part of the church not just in the future but in the here and now.

Rather than being "ghettoized" in youth groups and activities well beyond the time they cease to be adolescents, it's important for them to be integrated into overall church life—early. Young people should be invited to participate in worship services, committees, and denominational work, including being hired for part-time and summer work where possible. The key criterion for greater participation should never be age, but rather competence.

A major concern for most of Canada's religious groups, of course, is that **the farm systems currently are shrinking.** There isn't much depth beyond the major league rosters. The reality is that

- fewer adults are actively involved than has been the case in the past;
- they consequently are not exposing their children to the churches on a level that matches their own parents and grandparents.

In dealing with their current numerical problems, many religious groups typically think that what they need to do is "get adults back to church." Quite obviously, they need to work hard at just that. However, such a reclamation strategy needs to be accompanied by simultaneous strategies aimed at **production** and **prevention**. In the course of working hard to enhance adult interest and involvement, it's important to ensure that those children and teenagers who are currently involved are not lost by the groups. **Ministry to and with youth and children is an absolute must.**

Shrinking farm systems		
	1975	1990
All adults		
attended regularly as children	51	39
attend weekly at present	31	23
Adults with school-age children		
attended wookly as children	48	41
attend weekly at present	32	26
children attend regularly	35	28

Tracking affiliates

Baseball teams don't just develop good farm systems. For decades they probably have led professional sports in their obsession with keeping detailed statistics on virtually every aspect of personal and team performance.

Churches would be wise to learn something about record-keeping from baseball. Having begun to create affiliates in the form of children and young people, **it is critically important for religious groups to know who these people are, and to stay in lifelong contact with them.**

As things stand, most groups fail to "track" affiliates in any systematic way. All too often, a family of members moves to a new home. The former congregation keeps their names on file for a few years. Sometimes, they make an effort to contact the former members, to see if they want to be kept on the rolls. Often, the former members have moved again, in the meantime. There's no way of getting back in touch. So they're simply dropped from the rolls. Unknown. Case closed.

Consequently, congregations typically lose touch with many of their members and adherents in a relatively short amount of time. Indicative of the poor record-keeping is the dramatic disparity between how many affiliates the census-takers tell groups they have, and how many affiliates they retain "on the books." Earlier we saw that the census-roll ratios typically range from about two to one to as high as five to one.

Statistics Canada estimates that the average Canadian makes a residential move about once every five years. For those of us who are learning to **"think affiliate,"** such a finding means that an average affiliate is changing addresses every five years. That translates into an awful lot of residential and geographical movement.

Going, going, gone

It has important implications for churches. **A residential move represents a new beginning, a fresh start.** A new address brings with it new neighbors, new friends, new schools, new stores, new ways of spending time, new outlooks. A residential move provides us with an opportunity both to embrace the new and discard the old—including some unwanted acquaintances, some bad habits, some unneeded involvements.

Residential movement is a major source of attrition for religious groups.

- Some 33% of Canadians who **didn't** make a residential switch during the period 1980 to 1990 said they were attending services weekly as of 1990.
- Among Canadians who **did** change addresses, the reported weekly attendance level was only 15%.[38]

In other words, **every time people move, about half of them will stop attending regularly.**

These findings suggest that **it is imperative for religious groups to become far more deliberate about keeping track of their geographically-mobile affiliates.** Far too many active members and nominal affiliates are being lost to the churches in the course of moving from place to place.

As I pointed out in *Fragmented Gods,* this plea is not a new one. Yet, tragically, it has fallen on deaf ears for far too long. Way back in 1903, the Committee on the State of Religion for the Baptist Convention of Ontario and Quebec wrote in its annual report, *Many whose names have been erased by change of residence have been lost sight of by the church where their membership had been. In connection with the losses by erasure, it is well to notice large numbers of non-resident members. ...Do not the foregoing statements demand on the part of our churches a more solicitous guardianship of those who have removed to other parts and have not united with the nearest Baptist church?[39]*

From the standpoint of both group resources and the well-being of affiliates, it is important that affiliates not disappear. As part of avoiding this disappearance act, **it's essential that religious groups keep track of their residentially-mobile members.**

A cause for pause? Statistics Canada and my own surveys document what we all know: the most residentially-mobile people in Canada are young adults.

- They are particularly on the move to pursue education, career, and family life.
- They also are the age whose disappearance has the most pronounced impact on religious group numbers. Active affiliates as a whole don't randomly "drop out;" total numbers decline because smaller numbers of young affiliates are produced and retained.

One of the key reasons why young people disappear from churches is that they frequently "slip between the cracks" as they move from place to place.

Some will object that, "If people—including young adults— really want to be involved in the churches, they will seek out a congregation on their own." Sometimes, but sometimes not. The old congregational experience colors the inclination to be involved in a new congregation.

Expressed in cost-benefit terms, people will not bother if the perceived benefits of involvement in the new setting are outweighed by the perceived costs of having been involved in the old setting. Churches in new locales therefore frequently have something of "a selling job" to do, in recruiting actives as well as in beginning to connect with marginal and inactive affiliates.

On the positive side, a residential move signals not only a new beginning not only for people but also for churches. In keeping track of people on the move, a new congregation has the opportunity to demonstrate the church's interest and merits, along with a willingness to respond to real wants and needs.

What currently is haphazard needs to become systematic.
- When tracking is done, it is usually for highly valued, active members. News of such moves is typically relayed via a conversation, a phone call, or a letter.
- Tracking needs to be far more extensive, reaching well beyond actives and highly valued members to include marginals, inactives, disaffiliates, and even unaffiliates.

Why? Because **it's important that churches have continuous, ongoing ministry to people who are identifying with them.** The only way that such continuity is possible in the face of widespread residential movement is for groups to develop first-rate means of staying in touch with affiliates.

Very few—if any—Roman Catholic, Mainline Protestant, or Conservative Protestant groups are currently doing much of this. Such groups would do well to take some strategy pages from the book of the Latter Day Saints—who not only recognized the need for such a tracking system, but have also mastered the process. LDS friends playfully lament that, "It's hard to hide from the Mormons." One friend who recently made a residential move said that she was contacted no less than three times within about six weeks.

The same "lament" is **not** heard very often by geographically-mobile Anglican, Baptist, United, or Roman Catholic affiliates. It should be.

When I presented some of these findings on residential mobility and attendance drop-off to sociology colleagues at a conference in San Diego in 1994, the obvious question was asked: when it's so important for religious organizations to keep in touch with people on the move, why have they been so slow to do so? After all, if people contribute time and money to a specific congregation, surely it's in the denomination's best interests not to lose touch with them when they move to another part of the city or country.

That last sentence identifies one key root of the problem: did you notice it? It's in the best interests of **congregations** to recruit new members, but it's not necessarily in their own personal best interests to help the **denomination**—and therefore some **other** congregation—retain departing members. Self-interest and limited resources may be combining to sabotage successful tracking.

Clearly congregations have to be willing to participate in tracking affiliates both for the good of the people involved, **and** for the collective good of groups involved in ministry. In a literal sense, "what goes around may come around." Effective ministry requires some short-term generosity for the good of all.

How the Mormons do it

The key to record-keeping lies with a centralized database that is located at church headquarters in Salt Lake City. The database includes the names of all members, along with relevant data. Responsibility for updating the information on members lies with each ward (congregation). A clerk is appointed who keeps Salt Lake informed of any record changes that are required, such as marital status, death, and—of course—residence changes. Computerized printouts are made available to each ward on a six-month basis.

When a person moves, he or she typically informs the clerk or another leader. This information is forwarded to church headquarters in Salt Lake City, and the church passes on the updated record to the new ward. When a member does not give notice of a move, the ward clerk attempts to find out the new address. If these attempts fail, Salt Lake is advised that the member's whereabouts are not known. At that point, the church—from its Utah headquarters—actively tries to locate the member. Methods include following family leads, or contacting the clerk in the ward where relatives, for example, are members.

If "misplaced" members show up in a new ward at some point, church headquarters is advised, and their membership record requisitioned. Some who have "fallen between the cracks" are discovered by missionaries in the course of their house-to-house visits.

It's not a perfect system, but it is constantly being improved.

—*Provided by LDS members Armand L. Mauss*
and Richard Humphreys

Generating the information

Thanks to modern technology, efficient means of keeping track of "affiliates on the move" are readily available. Religious groups therefore need to adopt means that enable them todo three things:

- generate information on residentially-mobile affiliates.
- distribute that information to local, "host" congregations.
- establish and maintain a superb record system.

There obviously are many ways in which records might be kept, varying with resources, church polity, extent of cooperation, and so on.

The important thing is that groups find ways of accomplishing the affiliate-tracking task. How they do it is up to them.

Perhaps ideally, the process begins with a religious group creating what amounts to a master file of all of its active and marginal affiliates, beginning with their children. Over time, as people became known, inactive affiliates and disaffiliates would also be added to the file. For purposes of coordination, a national affiliate office might be established.

For those skeptics who think this all sounds rather sly and even ethically questionable in an age when people are wary of groups, companies, and government departments that "have them on file," I'd point out that what I am talking about is fairly limited and innocuous data, primarily demographic in nature. Any other information would probably pertain to the nature of an affiliate's relationship to the group. I offer a possible example in FIGURE 4.1.

Ideally, this **affiliate record** would be placed in the files of the local congregation, with a copy submitted to "the national statistics office" or some kind of counterpart. Through such procedures, it would be possible over time to assemble a comprehensive—if not total—list of affiliates.

Yes, it would be asking a lot of local congregations. And, again, I would emphasize that "the benefits" are in terms of individuals and the whole church, rather than necessarily direct "gains" for cooperating congregations. However, as churches became more and more convinced of the long-term and collective value of such record-keeping, cooperation undoubtedly would become easier to obtain.

I admit that such a complete census of affiliates is probably a shade elusive in most of our lifetimes. But keeping track of geographically-mobile affiliates is not. While the precise details of imple-

FIGURE 4.1
A sample Affiliate Record

```
Name_____

Address_____

Phone: Area Code _____Number _____

Gender     1  Male      2  Female

Age     1  under 15   2  16–19   3  20–24   4  25–29   5  30–39

        6  40–49      7  50–59   8  60–65   9  over 65

Marital status   1 Married     2 Never married    3 Separated

                 4 Divorced    5 Cohabiting         6 Widowed

Children    0     1     2     3       4 or more

Ages        ___ under 6 ___ 7–12 ___ 13–15 ___ 16–19

            ___ 20 & over

Affiliate status  1  Active  2 Marginal  3 Inactive  4 Disaffiliate

                  5  Non-affiliate

Congregation _____

Address _____

Contact person _____

Phone: Area Code _____Number _____

COMMENTS (if any)

_____

_____
```

mentation can vary, some points are clearly generic.
- Cooperation among a religious group's congregations is essential.
- A coordinating national office—or at least some contact point—needs to be established, to which congregations can send information on residentially-mobile affiliates.
- A person within each congregation perhaps could be given the responsibility of looking after the task, with congregational participation monitored on an ongoing basis by some denominational mechanism.

- The relaying of information would have to be extremely "user-friendly." One possibility is the use of a simple prepaid post card containing the name of the person or persons on the move; a fax machine might be better; a 1-800 number even better still.

The "card" or "memo" might be as detailed as the record example given in FIGURE 4.1; it also might be considerably briefer.

The procedure would be something like this:
1. Information would emerge that an affiliate is moving or has moved.
2. The address of destination would be obtained.
3. The "mobility card" would be filled out, and sent to the group's national office.
4. The national office would retain a copy (see, I'm still pulling for that national census ideal), and send the information on to the church or churches in the new locale.

This last step requires some clarification and caveats.

Counting "Assists" as well as "Goals"

Perhaps local congregations could establish a kind of performance index for "affiliate relocation." That is, they should pride themselves on how many of the members who have moved away have found themselves a comfortable new church home—regardless of what denomination. The "sending" church should not rest, but consider the task a part of its ongoing ministry, until the members who have moved are, in fact, comfortably settled. The current pattern seems to be to wish them well, push them out of the nest, and trust that they can fly. Sometimes—often—they can't.

Perhaps a congregation's annual report could include, along with the statistics on births and deaths, baptisms and marriages and funerals, a few lines something like this:

Number of members transferred out   _____
Number of new congregational homes found   _____
Success ratio   _____%

—Jim Taylor, Wood Lake Books

Distributing the data

When only one church of a denomination is found in a given community, the denomination would obviously relay such information only to that congregation. Somewhat more complex—and potentially divisive—is how to disseminate information when a large number of churches are found in major urban areas, including congregations which openly define themselves as regional or even city-wide churches. We don't want to see all of this degenerate into a mobile-member "peanut scramble."

Given the importance of resolving such issues, denominations and congregations have to be committed not to magnifying the difficulties but to engaging in creative problem-solving. The alternative? Residentially-mobile affiliates will continue to disappear.

- One possibility is to have such issues resolved at local denominational ministerial levels.
- A member's previous congregational type—such as a regional church versus a neighborhood church—might be a consideration in "assigning" affiliates.
- Flexibility and commitment to connecting with affiliates have to be primary considerations; if one congregation fails to make headway, for example, other congregations that might be able to relate more effectively to a given affiliate need to be given the opportunity to do so.

Sure I'm dreaming; sure I know that I am thinking idealistically. But frankly, the alternative to dreams and ideals is to continue doing what we are doing now. And that's a sure recipe for going down the tubes! If churches are to connect with Canadians in need of ministry, **we have to pursue what can be, rather than settle for what is.**

A closing point. Efforts to "create" and "track" affiliates will frequently have as their most visible result the creation and retention of people who are actively involved in the churches—the core of the most highly socialized and committed members. Critics might note that, in practice, such a process will, at least initially, contribute primarily to a much-improved method of "circulating the saints."

They're probably right. But that's not exactly a bad thing. Rather, it is an important facet of ministry to larger numbers of uninvolved affiliates. **More effective ministry "to the saints" translates into an increase in the size of the resource base that is absolutely essential if ministry of any kind is to take place.** These people are the life-blood of religious groups that aspire to reach out to other Canadians. They need to be coveted and kept. To let them slip away in the course of residential moves is irresponsible and unnecessary—not to mention extremely costly.

Creating and tracking need not, however, be limited only to active members. Ideally (there goes that word again) marginals, inactives, and disaffiliates would be "tracked" as well, in order that efforts to engage in ministry might take place over their lifetimes.

Currently, a major problem is that most of these "least active" affiliates are largely unknown to the churches. That situation, however, can fairly easily be changed.

*"The Son of Man came to seek and
to save what was lost."*
—Luke 19:10

Chapter 5
Locating lost affiliates

Last night, after penning the last few lines of chapter 4, I went to bed. Before turning out the lights, I continued my reading in the Gospel of Luke. And in the early morning hours, I arrived at these familiar lines:

"Which one of you, having a hundred sheep and losing one of them, does not leave the ninety-nine in the wilderness and go after the one that is lost until he finds it? ...Or what woman having ten silver coins, if she loses one of them, does not light a lamp, sweep the house, and search carefully until she finds it?"[40]

The word "lost" has fallen into disfavor among many religious leaders these days. It has come to be synonymous with "lost souls," sounding like a harsh and judgmental putdown of people who do not conform to a very narrow concept of commitment—not exactly in tune with Canadian ideas about valuing diversity and recognizing religious mosaics.

- Demographically-speaking, however, "lost" is an accurate description of the relationship of large numbers of affiliates to the groups with which they identify. They literally have become "lost" in the denseness of the Canadian population.
- Groups don't know who they are or where they are. They are like the missing sheep or misplaced money of which Jesus spoke.
- Spiritually-speaking, significant numbers of Canadians are "lost" in the sense that they are looking for purpose and meaning. A good many are exclaiming, "There's got to be more!"—but they're not sure where the answers lie. In Jesus' parables, they are like sheep that need to be found, money that needs to have its value realized.

If religious groups are to minister not only to the initiated but also to countless thousands of additional people who require ministry, they have to locate their "lost" affiliates. The difficulty involved in finding the lost has been grossly exaggerated. They can be found with relative ease.

Finding affiliates

Unless I'm missing something, it's not the job of the sheep to go looking for the shepherd. To put it bluntly, the onus for churches and Canadians connecting lies with the churches.

There are essentially two basic strategies to locate "misplaced" affiliates:

- census surveys, and
- cataloguing them through contact.

The religious census

One strategy is to carry out a door-to-door census, literally asking everyone in a given area to volunteer religious affiliation information. It's like the census that took Mary and Joseph to Bethlehem, except that you go to the people instead of expecting the people to come to you. Where people claim no religious tie, you probe for religious memory, by pursuing parental or guardian identification.

A true census gathers information on **everyone** in a community. It gives you the affiliation of each individual. A sample survey, by contrast, will give you information only about **some** of the people. Combined with analyses of census tract data from Statistics Canada, a sample will provide useful information about the general characteristics of a given area.

Because churches typically draw people from outside their immediate communities—especially in urban areas—there's a need to make sure that surveys aimed at uncovering affiliates are not limited only to one community. Regions and (where possible) even entire cities need to be surveyed to ensure blanket coverage.

Let no one be misled here: regardless of scope, door-to-door surveys are hard work. They are time-consuming, and require a large number of people who are well-trained. Consequently, they are best conducted in cooperation with other religious groups in a community, region, or city who also recognize the merits of gathering such data.

If there is anything that my surveys over the years have taught me it's that everyone thinks they know how to do a survey. The result is an awful lot of awful surveys.

Affiliate surveys require the technical input of people with survey research expertise. Without guidance, religious groups might encounter a number of basic problems, such as the following.

- The **interviewer's introduction** is very important. In probing affiliation, one has to stay neutral while at the same time being ethical about who one is. For example, saying one is "doing a survey on behalf of the Central Pentecostal Church" might result in a fast termination of the interview; saying one is "conducting a brief survey on behalf of the York Council of Churches" has a much better chance of proceeding.
- The **interviewer's demeanor** is critical. People need to be trained about how to act and even to look. One "bad interviewer" will not only have difficulty obtaining information; he or she can do considerable public relations damage.
- The **length of the survey** must be short. Time will typically be very limited. One has to ask very little, yet obtain the information required.
- The **survey items** have to tap precisely what churches want to know.

I do not raise these points either to discourage the carrying out of surveys—or to generate business for researchers like myself! These issues can be resolved. But it's important that they be anticipated so that they can be addressed. In some instances it may be wise to consider "farming" the entire survey project out to a university or research company. Clearly costs and benefits have to be weighed.

Because of the resources required, it is highly advantageous—as I mentioned—for various groups to work together in carrying out a census of affiliates. In addition, precisely because people identify with a wide range of groups, diverse participation helps to give the project legitimacy. Still further, the willingness of a variety of groups to engage in collective ministry offers further possible "spin-off benefits" in the form of heightened morale and greater solidarity.

Having located their affiliates within a given area, the groups compile the information and then make it available to each other. While distribution of the affiliate information obviously would vary with agreements, one option is simply to give Anglican data to Anglicans, Roman Catholic to Catholics, information on Baptists to Baptists, on Jews to Jews, and so on. Cooperating groups have to decide among themselves as to how they wish to distribute the non-affiliate, life-long "nones."

The major advantage of a survey census? Significant affiliate pools are uncovered almost overnight, enabling congregations to begin to engage in the most challenging and rewarding stage of the exercise—making contact and exploring ministry.

To recap:
- A survey to uncover affiliates is a full religious census of a given area.
- Cooperation and involvement of the various religious groups in the area is highly desirable.
- Technical advice is a must.
- Faith groups—including those who did not choose to participate—are given the names and addresses of the people who identify with them. If people claim "no preference," parents' identification is used.

Following is a sample of an "interview schedule" that might allow groups to obtain the information they need on affiliates. While refusals will not be uncommon, another "problem" to keep in mind is the tendency of some people to want to talk in detail about their faith or views on religion. In the census survey, interviewers need to get the essential information, and move on.

The purpose at this point is data collection. Detailed dialogue and ministry is for another time.

Figure 5.1
A sample survey census

Hi! I'm calling on behalf of the West Vancouver Council of Churches.
(Clarify what the council is, if necessary.)

We're doing a very brief religious census of the community today, to find out something of the makeup of the area. I assure you that I am not trying to persuade you to do anything as part of this survey. I'd like to ask you just two very quick questions, if I could; I'll only need less than a minute.

1   Refused   2   Able to Proceed

1. Do you have a religious preference, such as Protestant, Catholic, or some other faith?

1   Yes, Protestant

   What denomination might that be? _____

2   Roman Catholic

3   Other Faith _____

4   No, I don't have any religious preference

If "No"

When you were growing up, did your parents or guardians have any particular religious preference?
1   Yes, my MOTHER was_____   2   No
1   Yes, my FATHER was _____   2   No

2. And could I please have your name?
Name _____

Thanks very much for your time.

Record address _____

Comments (if any):

Cataloguing through contact

A very good alternative to the survey census needs to be considered when resources and situational factors make the full-scale survey approach of questionable value. Those who like biblical precedents need look no further than the parable of the lost coin that follows the parable of the lost sheep. While the shepherd left the 99 sheep behind and went out looking for the one that was lost, the woman who lost the silver coin stayed put, lit a lamp, swept the house, and eventually found the coin right there.

A somewhat slower but nonetheless productive method of locating lost affiliates is to "stay put" and wait for them to surface.

- Research findings tell us that, over time, most affiliates will request rites of passage—christenings, baptisms, weddings, funerals, and the like. We're talking big numbers: about 75% of 15- to 24-year-olds say they will be looking to the churches for birth-related ceremonies, around 85% for weddings, and close to 90% for funerals.[41]
- Further, it's important to keep in mind that **less than 20% of Canadians say that they never attend services at all.** This means that the majority of marginal affiliates and inactive affiliates do show up in churches from time to time. They do attend, just not regularly—in some cases, not very often at all.

Marginals, inactives, disaffiliates, and non-affiliates who are encountered in these two ways need to be carefully catalogued; but thanks to their own initiatives, they can be found.

In addition to cataloguing people through rites of passage requests and occasional attendance, affiliates can be located by simple word of mouth—a process, incidentally, that is much easier and less expensive than conducting door-to-door surveys. People in the churches typically have a large number of friends and acquaintances who are uninvolved affiliates. If groups will consciously provide their active members with some opportunities for "affiliate brainstorming," considerable information can be gathered. One member might say, "My next door neighbors are Presbyterian; the couple beyond them come from Estonia, so they're probably Lutheran..."

Cataloguing through contact can be a very effective means of finding affiliates, although it obviously is not as complete a method as the survey census. Still, the good news is that, via either method, large numbers of affiliates **can** be located.

And don't forget that, at the same time that they are surveying and/or cataloguing, congregations will be receiving a constant stream of names of affiliates who have moved into their areas—through other groups working hard at keeping track of people who have been moving from place to place.

It's an attainable dream. Yes it is! Systematic efforts to track and locate affiliates can result in thousands and thousands of uninvolved affiliates being found.

Classifying affiliates

In calling on churches to **"think concentric,"** I've been stressing what you already know well: when it comes to churches, there clearly are considerable differences in the interest and involvement levels of affiliates.

In attempting to relate to affiliates, it therefore is essential to distinguish between them. I've been suggesting that a helpful procedure might be to start by acknowledging their differences in involvement levels. Using attendance as our measure, I identify the following broad categories:

- **Active affiliates**...attend almost every week or more.
- **Marginal affiliates**...attend twice a month to several times a year.
- **Inactive affiliates**...attend about once a year or less.
- **Disaffiliates**...don't identify, but have parents who do.
- **Non-affiliates**...don't identify; parents did not as well.

Some preliminary reflecting on the five categories suggests that strategies would differ considerably depending whether one's primary goal was "getting people out to church" or ministering to their needs.

- If one wants to pack the pews, the geographically-mobile actives are the people to pursue, followed by the marginals. Both categories can be expected to be reasonably receptive to contact and to overtures to become involved. The marginals, by definition, would require more work.
- If service is a primary goal, inactives and even disaffiliates would seem to be categories that could be targeted. In both instances, the major hurdle may well be convincing these uninvolved affiliates that the church has something worthwhile to offer them.

Affiliates differ considerably from one another. **The diversity of affiliates needs to be clearly recognized if effective strategies for relating to them are to be developed.**

Affiliates are a varied bunch

Some fascinating parallel work on people on the edges of church life is being carried out in the United States by two close friends and colleagues, Kirk Hadaway and Penny Marler.[42] They differentiate four main types of "marginals":

- **Traditionalists** do not attend more often primarily because they are unable to do so; health and job hours, for example, are key factors.
- **Liberals** see churches in fairly positive terms, but are not inclined to hold traditional beliefs; they tend to hold fairly liberal social and political views and are satisfied with their current level of attendance—although most say they want their children to receive religious instruction.
- **Lifelongers** have been involved enough over time to feel that the church is valuable, but not enough to see it as having a critical place in their lives.
- **Critics** find services boring and feel churches are neither doing a particularly good job in addressing justice issues or helping people find meaning; most were active when they were younger, but question the value of churches at this point in time.

Similarly, in examining "inactives," they distinguish at least three main types:

- The **Estranged** have had a falling out with the church or may simply feel "burned out"; while they tend to value faith and feel committed, they have found reasons not to attend. In a survey they may come across as "hostile."
- The **Indifferent** are not antagonistic toward the church—they just don't care. Religion is not very important to them. Their choice not to attend more often is based on their sense that there is no particular reason to do so.
- The **Nominals** hold on to an affiliation label but to little else. They learned an uncommitted form of faith early in life and now have few traditional beliefs. Their values are self-made, and ongoing identification appears to be primarily for cultural and family reasons.

In tangible terms, once an affiliate has been located, **the next step is for a congregation to make contact.** Here a personal visit from a minister or church leader is essential. The primary purpose of this initial contact is to clarify the affiliate's relationship to the church and the faith. For purposes of ministry, affiliates need to be classified, using a scheme such as I am proposing—**actives, marginals, inactives, disaffiliates,** and **non-affiliates**—or something similar.

Obviously, flexibility and sensitivity have to be used in attempting to "sort" affiliates. The point is, however, that it is necessary to be cognizant of their "distances" from active involvement and commitment, in order to determine how to relate most effectively to them. "Thinking concentric" will determine, for example,

- how affiliates should be approached,
- what types of ministry are required, and
- what kinds of time-lines are involved.

Affiliates can be created. They also can be fairly readily tracked, located, and their variations acknowledged. What is required is for religious groups to establish appropriate policies, programs, and procedures.

But now, having located these affiliates—somewhere around 50% of the Canadian population—the next question facing religious groups is the toughest of all: **what do they want to do with them?** That question makes an additional question necessary: what are religious groups **able** to do with them?

To this vitally important question of ministry we will now turn.

*"Jesus went throughout Galilee,
teaching...preaching...healing.
Large crowds followed him."*
—Matthew 4:23-25

Chapter 6
Ministering to affiliates

We've been fooling ourselves. We've acted as if it's a difficult task to "find lost sheep," and have maintained that's why we haven't been able to do things like minister to people and engage in evangelism. Let's face it—it's been pretty easy to huddle together in sanctuaries and meeting rooms and decry our inability to reach uninvolved and disinterested Canadians.

However, the ready access to strategies that make it fairly easy for us to find those affiliates has blown our cover. **The real problem isn't locating affiliates; it's knowing what to do when we find them.** Maybe that's why we've been so slow to look.

It's like the old story of being out with Dad on our first fishing trip. Having reached the point where we just got comfortable with the boat and the bait, that profound question dawned on us: "By the way, Dad, what do I do if I catch a fish?"

It's the kind of question Anglicans in the New Westminster Diocese found themselves raising when they embarked on the advertising campaign I talked about in *Unknown Gods.*[43] Led by communications officer Lorie Chortyk, they developed imaginative posterads, encouraging people who "think they are Anglicans" to "Show your spirit" and "Come back to church." Having gotten excited about the campaign and put their 1-800 number in place, they then—says Chortyk—found themselves asking the real tough question: "But what if someone calls?"

The major problem is not **access**; it's **performance**. Now that we've got their attention, what do we do? Now that they are listening, what do we say?

Once affiliates have been located and churches have an opportunity to relate to them, it seems to me that five basic guidelines are essential to effective ministry.

 ## Be clear about what you want to accomplish

It's not my job as a sociologist to tell you what your objectives should be. **But have some objectives.** Be clear about what it is that you want to see happen, what it is that you are trying to do.

I sometimes get the sense that more than a few congregations are living on the momentum of commitment to some long-forgotten purpose. People at some point, way back when, had a dream as to what they wanted the church to be. But somewhere along the way, the dream evaporated and has not really been replaced. Members and ministers come and go, and the church just keeps on ticking. It's not clear that anyone knows particularly why—maybe they don't care why, as long as the church serves the needs of its active core of members.

Unfortunately, **congregations that are running on some kind of unidentified inertia are not likely to be able to offer inactive affiliates very much.** Over and over again, experts today tell organizations that they need to be clear as to "what business they are in"—what they are about. Churches that can minister to uninvolved affiliates need a clear sense of what they are trying to be and do.

It's important to remember that activity is not purpose. Almost all groups typically have a wide variety of programs and events on the books. Often, these are so abundant that they literally jostle for space and special insert coverage in bulging weekly bulletins. Significantly, ministers frequently acknowledge that "what's going on" seems often to reflect conventional congregational activities and the personal interests of the membership, rather than necessarily being informed by some clear, integrating sense of purpose.

Take visitation programs, for example. Some congregations have members contact people in a neighborhood who are not involved in any church. Why? I'm not so sure that the groups themselves are all that sure why. If asked directly, members participating in the effort would probably say that they "hope to get people out to church."

That's not necessarily a bad goal; nor is it necessarily a good one. But it needs to be clearly understood, because of the implications it has for how a church will relate to affiliates.

Generally speaking, there seem to be three major kinds of objectives that churches have in mind when they are dealing with people "on the outside."

- **Evangelism**—the goal of a person coming to profess Christian faith.
- **Recruitment**—the goal of a person becoming more involved in a church, through attendance, membership, and personal and financial participation.
- **Service**—the goal of addressing a person's spiritual, personal, and social needs.

A leader calls evangelicals to do more

Ever since he walked the earth, Jesus has inspired radicals from the Apostle Paul and Francis of Assisi to John Knox and Martin Luther and others.

Today I'm looking for genuine contemporary radicals. And I don't mean religious lunatics who, in absurd or obnoxious style, attract attention. I remember too well, as a teenager in Saskatoon, being embarrassed by a "Christian" group who arrived in town and quickly landed in the local jail. They said it was because they were evangelizing. In fact they drove up and down 2nd Avenue, screaming Bible verses. They got what they deserved while we slipped away, hoping no one one would associate us with them.

What I'm looking for is more than noticeable behavior. Out of our emerging generation we need women and men who will upset the status quo of conventional, complacent, secular thought and be authentic, biblically-based radicals. Too often evangelicals simply stand on the sidelines expecting Roman Catholics, such as Mother Teresa, or Mainline Protestants to defend the defenseless. We must understand that to bring about change, it will take more than a few powerful sermons or pamphlets. It takes carefully constructed and funded strategies. It also calls for churches, together in communities, to share human and fiscal resources.

I hear much about AIDS. But where are those who will bring healing and the love of Christ to those facing the final moments of life? I hear many decry the cost of taxes and government programs. But I see few crafting plans to help the homeless find somewhere to live.

I find myself longing, not for the past, but for a new breed of Christians who will rise above the narcissism and ego-centered theology of our new-Evangelicalism and live out Christ's righteousness.

—Brian Stiller, executive director of the Evangelical Fellowship of Canada.[44]

Congregations need to be in touch with how their efforts to minister to affiliates are motivated by these three goals. They need to be clear, for example, as to whether they are in the "church building" business or the "faith sharing" business, whether their primary objective is to "win souls," engage in service, enlarge their memberships—or something else.

2 Be clear about what you can offer

When asked about the nature of their ministry, **many congregations respond predictably that they are already doing it all.** In relating to affiliates and others, they are attempting to evangelize, encourage participation, and to serve.

That's well and good—in theory. However, if they want to get beyond rhetorical claims, **churches need to conduct what amount to very careful "product inventories" to see what they in fact are capable of offering to affiliates**. The danger, of course, is that in trying to do everything, they may not do anything particularly well. It might make much more sense to concentrate on being very good in one or more primary areas.

Specifically, given that the primary facets of Christian ministry lie in emphasizing God, self, and society—these three themes seem consistent with what uninvolved affiliates want and need—it's important for churches to ask themselves to what extent those three themes are actually present in their existing programs and activities.

For example, suppose that through a neighborhood affiliate survey—or a personal contact—things like this begin to happen. (And they will.)

- A Presbyterian minister makes contact with a young mother who is in the midst of a devastating separation, and requires emotional support, maybe some financial help, and possibly doesn't know quite what she is going to do with her three pre-school children while she looks for a job. "Things are pretty bad right now," she understates.
- "Hey, the timing is incredible," she says. "My husband and I moved here about six months ago and were just saying yesterday that we

would really like to start attending a Lutheran church. We're Lutherans, you know."

- He says that although he was raised a Mennonite, he is sick and tired of "religions that make us all feel guilty about everything." He has no interest in a church that can't "celebrate life" or isn't open to a wide range of spiritual expressions. He tells the "Community Church" pastor that he has been reading a lot of "New Age stuff" and is "into reincarnation and a few things you probably don't approve of." Still, as they talk, he admits, "My past isn't all that easy to get rid of—and I guess some parts of it weren't all that bad. Maybe I should catch one of your services."

- "Glad you took the trouble to come by," says another affiliate in his mid-30s. "I've really been feeling that something is missing in my life. Dad was Jewish—and that's what I feel I am, but Mom was really not very interested in religion. I wouldn't mind having some kind of ties with the synagogue—although I'm not quite sure what at this point."

- An Anglican priest, who has been wrestling with some of her own thoughts about life and death, visits a man in his early 40s who has called the church office. He was raised in an Anglican home, but hasn't attended for a number of years. His wife is dying of cancer—and he is desperately looking for meaning and hope. "I'd like to think there's more to it all than just this," he says. He pauses, then asks, "What do you think?"

- "Hey, am I glad to see you," she says to a somewhat startled United Church minister. "You're the one religious group that has shown some guts about us gays and lesbians. My partner and I have been looking for a church where we can feel welcome. Where did you say your church is located?"

- An evangelical pastor visits someone who "thinks" he is Nazarene, but is living with a female friend and uses pretty colorful language. But he says he has "really been thinking about God a lot lately," and, just as the pastor is leaving, takes him by surprise by announcing, "You know—you're different from the ministers I used to know; I think I'd like to come out to church this Sunday."

- She says that she "probably" made a mistake not getting "the kids" to church when they were small. But the fact of the matter is that her 15-year-old son and 13-year-old daughter are giving her fits. He's missing a lot of school and hanging out with a tough crowd— the police came to the house a couple of times in the past few months, responding to some complaints. Her daughter was okay until recently, but now she too has become "hard to handle," skipping school, and not coming home at all some weekend nights. Her husband is on the road most of the time, and she herself is working long hours. She knows she hasn't been "a very good Catholic," but actually found herself quite happy to hear the door bell ring and see—as she said with a laugh—a "young and sort of normal-looking" priest standing there. "Is there anything you can do to help me, Father?" she asks.

What would your church have available to offer these people? Is your standard-fare Bible study, women's group, or Christian Education program a suitable response in each case?

These illustrations, of course, represent only a small sampling of the diverse social, personal, and spiritual needs that are characterizing large numbers of affiliates. In some instances, the persons making contact come from congregations whose ministries enable them to have confidence that the needs of these kinds of people can be met. In other instances, they may know that it is going to be very difficult to come up with what is required.

As churches attempt to reach out and connect with their affiliates, and to respond to their needs and interests, they need to make sure that they know well what they are able "to deliver."

- Sometimes they will be able to respond directly, using their own resources. They may be able to provide spiritual help, personal and relational counsel, opportunities for children and teenagers, some financial assistance.
- In many instances they will be able to respond, but the key will be their ability to draw on other community resources, including the resources of other religious groups.
- In still other situations, it will be important to acknowledge to oneself—and as soon as is possible to the affiliate as well—that "the fit" with one's congregation is not especially good. It will be equally important to know about other ministry options—another congregation, another minister, another denomination, even another faith—and to do everything possible to help to facilitate that fit.

In the course of determining what a church can bring, it's probably very helpful to conduct something of an "inventory" of congregational resources. The starting place might be **what is**—what a church has to offer with respect to the central God, self, and society **interests and needs** that are being expressed by large numbers of Canadian affiliates.

Sample church program inventory			
What we have	**What affiliates need**		
	God	Self	Society
Worship services generally	x		
Church school	x	x	
Music		x	
New member classes	x	x	x
Prayer group	x		
Bible study	x		
Social action group			x
Daycare			x
Men's programs		x	x
Seniors' programs		x	x
Women's programs	x	x	x
Youth programs		x	
Social events		x	x
Marriage counseling		x	x

Such evaluations will be extremely telling about what is, what is not, and what needs to be. (Incidentally, in case you missed it, there are more than a few holes in what this church has to offer...)

Inventories are not necessarily negative—just necessary. They need to be constantly evaluated and adjusted in the light of a third consideration—what affiliates require.

3 Be clear about interests and needs

If people who value faith think that religion can indeed speak to the full range of human needs, then it goes without saying that ministry requires a clear understanding of **when** to bring **what** to individual lives.

Jesus himself did not minister to people in a blanket fashion. He met different needs with different responses

- healing the sick
- feeding the hungry
- calming the distressed
- comforting the bereaved
- engaging the inquisitive
- debating the critics
- exhibiting anger and exhibiting tears
- decrying self-righteousness
- and being merciful to sinners.

According to the research, there's no doubt that Canadians have a wide range of relational, personal, and spiritual interests and needs. If churches are in touch with what their affiliates want and need, there is every reason to believe that at least many will be responsive to what churches have to offer.

The key here is that there has to be a good "fit" between what churches are doing and what people are needing. If churches are doing one thing and affiliates require another, no one should be surprised to find that people are not looking to religious groups for answers.

A quick analogy. These days, companies don't attempt to **persuade** people to buy their products; in this, the era of marketing, they attempt to **provide** people with what they want and need. The lines from the experts that endorse such a concept abound; I pulled some of them up in *Unknown Gods*.[45]

- "The aim of marketing is to make selling superfluous. The aim is to know and understand the customer so well that the product fits...and sells itself."
  —management theorist Peter Drucker.
- "Ask not what your consumer can do for you but what you can do for your consumer; winning over the consumer depends on how much extra you can actually deliver—the product, plus, plus, plus."
  —trends analyst Faith Popcorn.
- "Find wants and fill them"; "Make what you can sell instead of trying to sell what you can make"; "Love the customer—not the product."
  —generic bits of folk wisdom.

Now, for heaven's sake, don't get scared off by the marketing language. If you've been following what I've been saying so far, you know that I fully subscribe to a religion with integrity. The last thing in the world that I want people to do is sacrifice faith and give consumption-minded Canadians whatever they want. Critics, wherever you are, give me a break!

What is significant in all of this marketing thinking is **the importance of churches getting solidly in touch with the needs of affiliates,** and determining to what extent they can, with both integrity and enthusiasm, respond to them. If they can't, they would do well to give other churches that opportunity.

When churches are "in touch" with people, one indicator will be that affiliates will take notice. Remember that once people believed Jesus could address their physical, personal, and spiritual needs, Jesus found himself dealing with "multitudes." If there is genuine need out there in Canadian society, quality ministry will be reflected with quantity.

From the time of that first personal contact with affiliates who have been located, congregational leaders have to **listen** carefully to what kinds of interests and needs those affiliates are expressing.

As Hadaway and Marler remind us, those interests and needs vary considerably between and even within "the concentric categories": marginals, inactives, disaffiliates, and non-affiliates. What such people require—and perhaps even more important, **don't** require—needs to be understood, and, yes, literally catalogued, using guides such as the following (computer-friendly modifications can easily be made):

Affiliate needs inventory

```
Name     _____
Address  _____
Phone    _____
Status     1 Active      2 Marginal      3 Inactive
           4 Disaffiliate  5 Non-affiliate

Interests and needs

God      _____
Self     _____
Society  _____
Other    _____
```

The reason for the bookkeeping is quite simple: **there has to be constant interaction between what churches are doing and what people are needing.** Programs need to be modified; appropriate resources need to be pursued. The alternative? Churches will continue to fail to connect with the majority of their affiliates.

There are other ways of "getting a good read" on the needs of affiliates. Harvey Stevens, a policy analyst for the Province of Manitoba and an active United Church layman, has given considerable thought to how churches might better understand the needs, for example, of **marginal affiliates.** Following some time together in Winnipeg, he suggested that focus groups might be helpful. I've included his proposal.

Exploring needs using focus groups

Essentially, the proposal involves contacting, by phone and/or letter, all those on the congregational rolls who have not attended church during the last year or who have attended only once or twice. The initial contact would explain the purpose of the call and obtain background information on them required for the second stage.

The second stage would involve convening a series of focus groups to explore basic themes around people's views of the church, church-going, their religious beliefs, etc.

At the conclusion of the initial contact, people would be asked if they would attend a focus group. If they decline, an option would then be to ask them the focus group questions over the phone so that their views are not lost.

The purpose of the exercise would be to gain insights about why people do not attend church, what would have to be different about church in order for them to attend more frequently, and what they want/need from the church. This information then could be used by the church to decide what new initiatives it should be offering to these people. We would be quite clear to those we contacted that we are not trying to pressure them into attending more frequently and/ or to give money. We simply want to listen to them and hear their concerns.

—provided by Harvey Stevens

Needs assessment, of course, does not stop with individuals. Churches that are sociologically-minded know that, if lives are to be enhanced, **it's essential that people have healthy social environments.**

- Religious groups that want to contribute to the lives of their affiliates must attempt to clearly understand the ways in which various institutions and organizations in communities and cities are contributing or not contributing to the quality of life of their people.

• Efforts to enrich individual lives have to be sensitive to the social factors that shape the environments in which ministry is taking place. Responses to poverty and discrimination, for example, require an understanding not only of individuals but of social conditions and social policies that contribute to inequity. Such community assessments of resources and issues ideally are carried out collectively, through groups working together.

The tragedy of the current situation in Canada is that, to a disturbing extent, **neither** party seems to be making the connection. Large numbers of average Canadians are not associating what they are looking for with the churches, and a good many churches are not associating what they are capable of providing with what Canadians want.

The solution, it seems to me, lies with churches bridging the current gap, following existing affiliation lines to Canadians, and getting in touch with their interests and needs.

Will it all lead to more active members, greater resources, and healthier churches? Probably. But hopefully those things will be **a product of enhanced ministry** to more people who find churches to be worth their time, energy, and money.

Let's start by attempting to reach out and minister to needs. That's the way Jesus did things. There's every reason to believe that **congregations which are responsive to affiliates will in turn and in time be strengthened by them.**

4 Have on-going contact

From the first few pages on, I've been stressing the importance of the **"religion is relational"** finding. Few readers need to be reminded that, following an initial visit—ideally by a minister or other trained personnel—the best way to maintain contact with uninvolved affiliates is through people.

A varied cast, however, is required. Sometimes it will be a minister, but not always. Sometimes a better contact is a lay leader, or a friend, maybe an acquaintance, perhaps children or the friends of children.

The relational principle, however, needs to be combined with the concentric principle. Not everyone wants ongoing visits; in fact, some people might be downright negative about the prospect. It was interesting to observe in the national *Unitrends* study, for example, that only about one in four average United Church members said that being visited by people in the church is something that they regard as particularly important. And these are active and committed members!

For some people, especially the inactives who attend only a few times a year or less, on-going contacts that are not face-to-face—such as announcements and newsletters—might be preferable.

The dangers of being too friendly

In many stagnant churches, anonymity is next to ungodliness. The underlying assumption is that friendliness and Christian love can only be shown by showering attention on the visitor. The effort is meant to make the person feel welcome and special. Exit interviews, however, indicate that such attention is generally undesired and often causes the visitor to feel violated. Many people visit a church with trepidation, and with a desire to take things slowly. These cautious visitors often prefer to remain part of the woodwork for a while, acting as participant-observers, unobtrusive and unfettered. [Members of growing churches] do what [is] reasonable and necessary to make the visitor feel welcomed, but not cornered.

—*George Barna in* User-Friendly Churches, *p. 177*

What's needed is considerable sensitivity and above-average social skills. The initial personal contact should provide the minister or lay leader with a fairly good sense of what kind of future contacts will be most appropriate.

Keeping in mind the diversity of affiliates, some fairly common-sense generalizations might be helpful:

- **Active affiliates** who are "looking for a church home" undoubtedly need the personal touch. What is involved here is primarily recruitment.
- **Marginal affiliates** may be receptive to occasional visits. However, in view of their tendency to attend off and on, the mail may be not only effective but preferred. Their children and, in some

cases, church friends might provide good and natural liaisons.

- **Inactive affiliates** are not likely to be overly enthused about receiving regular house calls. But mailed announcements about programs and activities of interest and value to them might be helpful. Their children—if involved in some church activities—would provide a natural link.
- **Disaffiliates**, given their parental ties to the church, might be receptive to special events, and programs involving their children. Announcements may be one way of retaining contact.

The research suggests that, generally-speaking, uninvolved affiliates can be expected to surface mainly for rites of passage and special events. Given their religious memory, many should have some receptivity to seasonal worship services (Christmas concerts, Easter pageants), age-related activities (Children's Sunday, Vacation Bible School Night), and family-related occasions (Mother's Day, Father and Son Banquets). They may also show up, and be surprisingly willing to help, at bazaars, sales, and suppers.

The Apostle Paul's classic adage about being "all things to all people in order to win some" seems to be particularly good advice when it comes to dealing with affiliates. There is no one way of connecting with Canadians. Their diversity ensures that. Instead, centrally important principles such as **thinking concentric** and **thinking relational** need to be combined with lots of creativity in order for effective ministry to take place.

A Roman Catholic calls the church to get creative

Through the past centuries the church has made use of a variety of materials, mediums and period styles in order to better communicate the Word of God to the people of the world. It is now time to make use of electronics, microchips, magnetic and optical recordings, lenses and startling new light sources to better communicate this same message. For the church to remain mired in the centuries-old medium of print may now be seen as a neglection of the prime ministry of the church: bringing the good news of Jesus Christ to the world.

This required liturgical renaissance is no easy task for anyone involved, but it must be done if our generation is to pass on the flame of faith undiminished.

—Rudoph S. Daldin, Windsor

---

5 Do it together

Again let me stress the point: **If the country's churches are to connect with Canadians in a comprehensive way, they have to engage in cooperative, collective ministry.** Even if the "religious market" were totally open, no single group—with maybe one or two exceptions—would have the human and financial resources to connect with all the people who are receptive to and in need of ministry.

But the point is, the market **isn't** wide open. Consequently, no one group, even with virtually unlimited resources, could do the job. The problem is one of access. Identification translates into pre-set limits. Canadians simply are not very receptive to overtures from groups that are not "their own."

Pre-existing limits mean that congregations are literally throwing away their money and time if they attempt to connect with people with whom they have no affinity. Religious groups that insist on going it alone will waste a lot while gaining little.

Adding to such futile debacles, efforts to reach people who don't already identify with a group may be highly counterproductive. Botched evangelistic efforts in the form of indiscriminate distributions of books and videos may do nothing for public relations. Ironically, such ill-fated efforts may actually make outreach more difficult for other groups who are in a better position to relate to the same individuals.

But if collective ministry is a necessity, it is also potentially a tremendous asset. Canadians are highly diverse. While we have many common dreams and values, we nonetheless have extremely varied religious backgrounds, lifestyles, and needs. **The only way that diversity can be adequately addressed is through the availability of diverse religious resources.**

Beyond religious history, not every congregation can speak to people who
- come from different social classes,
- have different cultural backgrounds,
- have unorthodox or traditional lifestyles,
- hold conservative or radical beliefs,

- are experiencing success or experiencing failure,
- are old as well as young,
- are homosexual as well as heterosexual.

Through collective ministry, however, **diverse needs can be met with diverse resources**.

And let no one be mistaken—the collective resources of Canada's religious groups are very extensive.

- Despite sagging attendance, the number of people attending services across the country in an average single week (around 5 million) exceeds the number of fans the Blue Jays draw in an entire season—and the Jays annually lead the entire American League in attendance.
- No other sector in the country has as many volunteer workers; the number of people who give time free to the churches exceeds all charities and service organizations combined; they represent an extremely impressive collection of talent.
- McDonald's might have 2,000 franchise outlets across the country—but the United Church of Canada alone also has over 2,000; the total of "outlets" for religious groups as a whole might exceed 25,000.
- The value of church real estate is greater than the value of the holdings of Eaton's, Sears, Canadian Tire, Zellers, The Bay, and Wal-Mart combined!

As Carl Dudley has put it, "The importance of the local church is often overlooked by the public press. In their reporting on religion, the mass media seem preoccupied with the actions of extremists, trends reflected in the public opinion polls, and statements of leaders and national religious assemblies." What is often missed, he says, is the fact that "the majority of people in the United States and Canada have chosen to relate themselves to Christian faith through local congregations." The congregation, Dudley writes, "appears to have endless resources in its history and in the intricate relationships and diverse perspectives of those who are committed to it."[46]

Collectively, the resources of religious groups are even more impressive. When combined and used strategically to follow identification lines, much can happen. **Diverse resources directed at diverse needs can lead to greatly enhanced ministry in Canada.**

Take "lines of identification," for example. What I have been proposing is that groups follow obvious lines of affinity, starting with people who actually identify with them. Groups with which people **don't** identify will at best be tolerated; at worst they will be treated with hostility. Most won't even be given a chance.

In much the same way, not all congregations **within the same denomination** will be able to adequately relate to an affiliate. A given church may find that about the only thing it has in common with the person is a denominational name.

Into the One

The union of diversity
is the gathering
of the Many
into the
One
and the
sharing of
One with the Many.
—*Regina Coupar, Anglican visual artist*

Here is where **collective ministry**—within denominations—comes in. The very diversity of ministry in any major denomination makes it possible to relate to an extremely wide range range of people. If a given church finds itself unable to meet the needs of an affiliate, and knows that she or he might be better served by another minister or congregation, hopefully a referral to another congregation can take place.

Here's an example. In the early 1970s, West Ellesmere United Church in Scarborough, Ontario, under the leadership of Berkeley Reynolds, was fairly conservative and evangelical. Parkwoods United, just a few blocks away, leaned more towards the other end of the theological spectrum. Parkwoods gained a number of loyal and very committed members, who wanted, in my source's words, "a more liberal, laissez-faire theology." Presumably, a certain number also moved the other way. But, for the most part, these members had to make the decision to move on their own. Unfortunatly, neither congregation saw it **as a service to their disaffiliated members** to help them find a better match for their needs and interests. Things need to be different.

Some identification lines, as I mentioned earlier, are "tattered." They have deteriorated for a variety of reasons to the point that they are fragile threads. Here again, collective ministry needs to kick in. It may well be better to refer such individuals to another minister or group that is better positioned to deal with them.

The direction of movement is not always predictable.
- Sometimes people need a more liberal congregation, sometimes a more conservative one.
- There are times when groups feel that they cannot, with integrity, point people in a different direction; in other instances, groups can.
- The collective spirit does not always run both ways.

The research shows that affiliation lines are in place; it also shows, however, that **about one in ten uninvolved affiliates are open to replacing those lines.** Good ministry, like the rest of life, surely sometimes involves letting go.

And then there are those "tangled" lines of identification—vague ties because parents had different religious backgrounds, for example. I remember a young boy in an orphanage in Louisville once who—playfully or otherwise—described himself as a "Batholic." Experimentation over time can also lead to identification confusion.

These kinds of situations call for some "creative flexibility" on the part of religious groups which are attempting to engage in ministry. **Any one group, by itself, is going to run into serious limitations.** The unfortunate result is that affiliates who are not responsive to that group's overtures may simply fail to have their needs met anywhere.

It seems to me that the solution is again **collective ministry,** where clergy and members who value faith and service over recruitment and pew-filling **work together to help such people find ministries that can be meaningful for them.** Of course it's an ideal—but it needs to be pursued.

Collective ministry needs to be taking place **within** groups and **between** groups. Because affiliates are extremely diversified, the relative abilities of various congregations to respond to them have to be recognized.

In putting such ideals into action, denominations and their regional and local expressions need to do four things:

1. Adopt explicit policies regarding the necessity, value, and importance of engaging in collective ministry;
2. Develop procedures that make it possible for churches to cooperate with and complement one another in their handling of affiliates, such as recogizing their limitations and referring them to other churches;
3. Recognize and reward the complementary roles that different churches play in such an interdependent system;
4. Encourage and promote sharing of skills, facilities, and activities.

Effective collective ministry also needs to take place between groups. As we have seen, a concerted effort to connect with Canadians cannot stop with the cooperative efforts of single religious groups. Collective ministry has to take place **across denominational and faith boundaries** as well. Therefore, in moving from theory to practice, diverse groups also need four steps:

1. Endorse policies for collective ministry between groups.
2. Establish procedures for acting collectively—such as referring affiliates of other groups to those groups, and referring "expired" and "tangled" leads according to the best interests of affiliates;
3. Engage in cooperative ventures;
4. Draw on each other's expertise and areas of competence.

Underlying such collective efforts is the recognition that, just as there are limits to what any one congregation can do, so there are limits to what any single denomination can do. Collectively, however, religious groups represent a powerful force, capable of relating effectively to Canadians.

Yes—I've looked into the faces of enough people in audiences to know that more than a few of you who are still reading this book are thinking, "It sounds great but... this Bibby guy has got his head in the clouds. It just won't happen."

It has to happen. Sure, some congregations will be wary of other congregations, and some denominations won't be all that excited about working with others of different theological persuasions. Crossing faiths won't exactly be a breeze either. Agreement on the handling of affiliates won't always be easy; organizers will squabble over the dividing up of geographically-mobile actives, and groups won't always agree on how people identified through community surveys should be allocated.

It doesn't matter. Such problems, as with other problems we have discussed, can be overcome. The alternative is to continue having fragmented, incomplete ministries to Canadians.

The challenging and exciting task of connecting with Canadians is something that has to be done together, or it will not be done at all. We have to find a way to make collective ministry work.

Working with other faiths

When immigrants come to cities like Toronto and Vancouver, we have a turnabout from the conditions during the long era of Christian missions. Now the Western city with Christian roots welcomes religious forces and factors which have been, up to this point, alien and opposed to its own. The modern multicultural society has compressed time and space from a globe to a city.

As more and more historic religions gather together in the multicultural society, dialogue and the process of "crossing over" become increasingly valuable as means of sympathetically understanding one another's viewpoint, and of enlarging our own perspectives.

This process, of course, assumes that one is more interested in changing oneself than in changing the other. The key to this method is a spirit in which we recognize that the other, the alien, has something to offer.

—*Roland Kawano, Anglican priest currently working in multicultural ministries for the United Church.*[47]

Personal postscript

I started out in the ministry. When I became a sociologist, I thought that my days of official ministry were behind me—as did my disappointed mother who has taken the liberty of telling several dozen people over the years that her eldest son could have been "another Billy Graham." She still hopes I'm "going to turn out all right."

As I carried out my research into religion in those early, pre-1987 years, I did so thinking of myself primarily as a sociologist who simply wanted to carry out sound work and leave the implications for ministry to others.

But, with the publication of *Fragmented Gods*, things changed. No, contrary to occasional rumor, I didn't become a Christian because of the book. I have valued Christian faith consistently over my lifetime; my reservations have pertained to the significance of the church as a human institution, and have had little to do with constancy of faith, or the immense valuing of God.

Since 1987, indicative of the maverick ways in which God works, I feel that I have literally been called into a somewhat different kind of ministry, told to travel out beyond the academic community and interpret my work to the country's faith groups, to assist them in better understanding themselves, and to do what I can to make more effective ministry possible. My research since the mid-80s has further convinced me that the country and Canadians are in urgent need of what the churches potentially can bring.

After first just watching the game, and then suggesting a few plays from the sidelines, I now find myself shedding the warm-up jacket and asking for a bit more playing time.

- For about a decade now, religious groups, colleges, ministerials, and organizations across the country have been asking me to discuss my findings with them. I have been able to do that fairly comfortably.
- But they have asked for more. They have asked me to reflect on the implications of the findings for ministry. Increasingly, I have stepped out of my role as detached chronicler, and have tried to offer some ideas as to what it all means.
- It still hasn't been enough. People have asked me about tangible strategies. With some reluctance, I have taken another step away from pure research and attempted to identify a number of tangible strategies that might be considered in carrying out some specific tasks.
- Yet people still want more. Just about everywhere I go, there are some individuals who sit pensively with paper and pen in hand, waiting for me to tell them "what tangible strategies" they should use.

I know my limits, and I have reached my limits. Theirs is an impossible expectation. "Tangible strategies" for what? Every situation has its own characteristics. No one can provide "strategies" that will address the specific issues in the wide range of unique settings in which people find themselves. Yet I have been asked to "present my research and discuss related strategies" by groups that include pastors, denominational staff, church boards, and lay leaders; hospital staff, chaplains, and other caregivers; university and theological college boards, faculty, students, and chaplains; high school administrators, teachers, counselors, and students; and Christian politicians and interest groups. I might add that the religious requests have come from a wide array of Roman Catholic, Mainline Protestant, and Conservative Protestant groups, along with Seventh Day Adventists and Unitarians.

The reason for offering you that tedious listing is to show you something of the impossible task people want to put on my rather limited shoulders. Unless I'm missing something, it seems to me that groups and individuals that want to uncover appropriate "strategies" ultimately have to do much of the specific legwork themselves. If they sit back and wait for pontifications from experts, nothing very concrete is ever going to take place.

People who want to see things happen have to make them happen. They have to lay out their own specific tasks and then— drawing on general principles and the best available information— engage in energetic, imaginative problem-solving.

No one can do your problem-solving for you—not Reg Bibby, not some of the better-known high-paid "religious gurus" and other wise folk.

But, although we can't simply turn to a tried and true body of solutions, we **can** exchange some interesting and potentially valuable ideas. In engaging in our individual problem-solving efforts, we can benefit greatly from our hearing what other people have learned along the way. We can use all the good ideas we can get.

And so, let's take a breather—all of this has been pretty heavy. Then let's sit back with our coffee in hand, and listen to some of North America's top "religious gurus" in a brainstorming session.

Chapter 7

With a little help from our friends

Since approximately 1980, a growing number of people have emerged in North America who have built on social research and thought to provide church leaders with practical help in enhancing ministry. They have some important things to say about how churches should be responding to the times.

In trying to find creative ways of connecting churches and Canadians, let's listen to seven of these people. These are not book reviews, but samples of some of their ideas. Readers who find their thoughts to be helpful are invited to pursue their thinking in much more detail via their respective books.

Obviously, these authorities on church renewal have much more to say than I have been able to include in these pages. I have tried to be fair to their themes—that is, I have tried not simply to proof-text from their work to support my own conclusions. When I did these summaries, however, I was surprised at how many times their recommendations paralleled my own analysis.

I could have cited a number of Canadians. Bud Phillips, Marion Best, Joanne Chafe, and Don Posterski all come to mind. Both Marion and Don have books out—published by Wood Lake—that are well worth examining. The "gurus" that follow were chosen mainly because they're the ones I hear people talking most about.

The point of this "simulated brainstorming session" is to supplement what has already been said so far, to stimulate further thought and, above all, to help people put ideas into action.

LOREN MEAD
A new church for new times

Loren B. Mead, an Episcopal priest, is the founder and president of The Alban Institute of Washington, D.C. He has spent some 40 years involved in congregational life as a minister, researcher, writer, and resource person. What follows is drawn from his 1991 book, The Once and Future Church: Reinventing the Congregation for a New Mission Frontier, *and his 1994 follow-up,* Transforming Congregations for the Future, *both published by The Alban Institute Inc., 4550 Montgomery Avenue, Suite 433N, Bethesda, MD 20814 (Used with permission. Copyright © 1991 and 1994. All rights reserved.)*

Mead's work is especially aimed at mainline Protestants and Roman Catholics—groups that have been part of the informal religious "establishment" in the United States. His thinking consequently applies particularly in Canada to the United Church, Anglicans, Presbyterians, Lutherans, and Roman Catholics. He acknowledges that other groups, notably Conservative Protestants, may find some elements over- or under-emphasized, but he believes his observations have implications for them as well.

Congregations are Mead's primary interest. "For six decades now," he writes, "I have inhabited them, enjoyed them, been frustrated by them, earned a living from them, and tried to understand them."[48] He has great confidence in their capabilities, maintaining that they historically have played a centrally-important societal role—second only to the family—in providing people with meaning, purpose, and community. Moreover, Mead argues that even families "run into trouble if they lose their connection to religion—and value-bearing communities"—the kind of communities that he feels are virtually unique to congregations.[49]

Mead associates the post-1950s decline in the size and influence of churches, especially mainline Protestantism, with their failure to engage in ministry using forms and structures appropriate to our times. "Cracks in current systems of ministry," writes Mead, can be seen at four different levels.

● **Clergy** frequently lack a clear-cut sense of who they are and what

their roles are.
- **Laity** are encouraged to view themselves as engaged in ministry, yet their input into denominational decisions and positions is often limited and ministry outside of the church itself is seldom rewarded.
- **Executive staff** have decreasing budgets; they also are commonly viewed as giving insufficient attention to local concerns.
- **Congregations** frequently are unsure about their reason for being; even though the urgent need for imaginative, caring ministries to their communities is apparent, many laity and clergy are unclear about how to proceed.

Typically, says Mead, denominations have responded to changing conditions in three main ways:
- frantic efforts to recapture the eroded support, complete with restructuring, relocation of offices, and realignment of staffs—efforts that usually fail;
- holding steady and hoping for the best, versus building a more effective system;
- moving ahead into a new paradigm of mission, rebuilding and reinventing the church as they go.

The third response is his clear preference: "I assume that we have no viable alternative to this third option," he writes, "even though most denominational responses so far have been along the lines of the first two."[50]

A major change in how ministry is carried out needs to take place. Twice before in its history, he says, the Christian Church has had to reorder its understanding of itself and the world. He calls these understandings "paradigms."
- The **Apostolic Paradigm** came into being in the first generations after Jesus. It saw the church as an intimate community called to serve and care for a hostile world.
- With the fourth century, the **Christendom Paradigm** began to emerge. It saw Church and Society as one, mission as an enterprise in "far-off" places, congregations as parishes, membership as the result of birth.

The legacy of that Christendom Paradigm, Mead maintains, makes it difficult for the Church today to create a new, third paradigm, accompanied by new structures appropriate for ministry.

Mead calls for a "reinvention of the Church," acknowledging that it may take several generations. "We will not see the end of it," he says, "but we must begin now."[51] A fundamental feature of that new Church will see the mission frontier moving "from the far-off edge of the Empire to the doors of the local congregation."[52] Accordingly, resources will need to flow primarily **to** congregations, rather than **away** from them. The "reinvented church," says Mead, will be characterized by a trained laity, an equipping clergy, denominations directing resources toward congregations, and a theology with lay origins. In short, he envisions "a church turned on its head. Upside down."[53]

In the course of the Church being reinvented, Mead envisions that tension will arise around views of

- the church as a **committed** versus a **geographical** community,
- mission as **servanthood** versus **conversion**, and
- membership as **inclusive** versus **exclusive**.

Mead recognizes that pressure and opportunity for change are not the same for every congregation, and therefore calls for "innovators, people and groups who will take a stab at a new way with the freedom to fail." He says, for example, that denominations "must learn to encourage innovation and even fund it, rather than handicap and punish it... Our most important asset is the pioneer, the one—or the many—who is willing to break new paths."[55]

To look at today's turmoil and uncertainty, writes Mead, is to see not only "troubled waters" but also "the potential presence of God's healing powers." The situation in our day is such, he says, that "Never before have those in religious congregations had more—potentially—to give to the other structures of society."[56]

"A new church is being born," Mead writes. **"It may not be the church we expect or want."** God, he says, is calling for a newness of the whole world, not just the church, and "calling us to participate in that new creation."[57]

In his latest book, Mead acknowledges that the situation is, if anything, worse than people have thought. "We are in serious trouble that we will not get out of soon," he writes, adding, "When we get clear of this storm, our religious institutions may bear little resemblance to those with which we grew up."[58]

He calls Christians to ask what congregations are for. The answers, he suggests, lie in returning to our Christian roots. Congregations are "called to be communities that follow Jesus in bringing good news to the pain of the world."[59]

As members "identify their calls and are nurtured and sent," Mead says, "we will see the development of the apostolate of the future church."[60]

Mead acknowledges some major roadblocks. These include financial problems that have not yet been squarely faced, a failure to enfranchise the laity (preferring clergy-run churches), and a reluctance to change organizational structures.

He identifies two central tasks:
- "rebuilding the wall," whereby we "clarify what makes us different, so that we can undertake our vocation as apostles"; and
- "restoring the temple," engaging in conversation with God through worship and prayer.[61]

He concludes: "What lies ahead is a storm, indeed. The winds are strong, and we cannot know all that is to come. But in and through this storm, a transforming power is at work to build an apostolic church. To be called to participate in that transformation is our life."[62]

> **Mead's central emphasis on "pursuing a new paradigm of mission and rebuilding and reinventing the church as we go" seems particularly pertinent to those who are serious about exploring new ways of connecting churches and Canadians. A number of his specific emphases also are important: locating ministry in committed congregations, seeing "the mission frontier" outside the doors of the local church, being willing to experiment, and recognizing that churches are well-positioned to make significant contributions to national life.**

BILL EASUM
Back to the future

In his role as director of Texas-based 21st Century Strategies, William Easum is a full-time consultant to religious groups and congregations in both the United States and Canada. He is a former United Methodist Church minister and well-known author. The following material is based on his book, Dancing With Dinosaurs, *published by Abingdon Press (Copyright © 1993. Used by permission.)*

Easum declares that, after about two centuries of efficient ministry, many North American churches today have become irrelevant to a hurting world. "All around are unchurched, hurting people," he writes. But many churches "refuse to change their methods and structures to minister to people where they are in ways they can understand."[63]

While major shifts are taking place in North American life, many churches, he says, look increasingly like dinosaurs. It's not just that they are failing to shift with the times. They also have voracious appetites, using most of their resources to feed themselves rather than to feed the unchurched. Such churches, he predicts, will eventually go the way of the dinosaur.

"God is calling us to find new ways to apply the good news to a new emerging world," writes Easum.[64] It is not the **substance** of the gospel that needs to be changed, but rather **how the gospel is packaged and proclaimed**. What is needed, according to Easum, are new paradigms for ministry. He provides this helpful definition of the term as he uses it: "A paradigm is a set of assumptions, beliefs, ideas, values, or expectations that form a filter through which we make meaning out of life, create structure and process, view information, and make value judgments."[65]

The paradigm he himself offers makes 12 assumptions, four of which are explicitly theological.

1. North America is the new mission field.
2. Society will become increasingly hostile to Christianity in the 21st century.

3. The distinction between clergy and laity will disappear in the next century.

4. If churches only improve what they have been doing, they will die.

5. The best way to fail today is to improve yesterday's successes.

6. Bureaucracies and traditional practices are the major causes of decline of most North American denominations.

7. Congregations that thrive in the next century will institute radical changes before the end of this century.

8. A way will be found to avoid world ecological and economic disaster.

9–12. **God** exists and creates everything; **Jesus Christ** is the center of human life; the **Bible** is our primary source of faith and practice; the purpose of **the church** is to bring the world to faith in Christ.

There is a great need, says Easum, for congregations to differentiate between their present practices and their Christian roots. He maintains that "the new world of the 21st century may be new to us, but it is not new to our spiritual ancestors. They developed Christian community in the midst of a very similar culture."[66]

"Based on the example of the early Christian communities," writes Easum, "the only way forward for congregations today is by turning outward to the world."[67] Leaders need to focus the congregation on the world rather than themselves.

Easum argues that the church's primary task is "to win the world to faith in God through Jesus Christ." Accordingly, nurturing members for the sake of those members alone is not the mission of the church, nor is the goal ever simply "to run the church." Every church should be growing or contributing to growth.

The issue is not size but ministry. He writes, "The person who is concerned about quality versus quantity needs to read the Acts of the Apostles. The Bible never pits the two measures against each other... And nowhere do I read that integrity has to be sacrificed in order for Christianity to grow."[68]

● A congregation that cannot grow because of its **location** can
   1. move to a new location;
   2. join one or two other congregations, selling properties and

starting a new congregation;
3. stay where it is and help start a new congregation in another area.
- A congregation that wishes to **remain small** can
  1. send members out to start a new congregation somewhere else;
  2. provide resources to help start new congregations.
- Very **old, small congregations** can
  1. reach out to nursing homes;
  2. do work at home for other congregations that are growing;
  3. send money to help start new congregations.

The clue to ministering to outsiders, Easum suggests, lies in turning, not to those who cling to the status quo, but to "people on the fringe of normalcy" who are developing nontraditional ministries. Such people study available information, look outside their organizations to discover what kind of ministries they need to develop, and promote excellence and innovation.

A number of major developments, he says, are characterizing effective "fringe ministries."

1. **Small group ministries replace programs.** They take the form of Bible study and support groups, with the most effective being cell-based groups.
2. **Pastors equip persons rather than doing ministry.** Teaching and preparing laity for ministry in the world is becoming more important than performing ministry on behalf of the church. In some instances, well-trained, bivocational, nonordained persons are replacing ordained clergy.
3. **Worship is being reformed.** The focus is God, the mood is celebrative, the music is in touch with the culture and moreover *is* the ritual; the service is entertaining, preaching is energetic and the message useful, dress is casual.
4. **Buildings are not important.** Multiple sites are increasingly common; money is invested in staff and ministry; neighborhood and geographical names are avoided, as are references to denomination and even the term "church."
5. **Weekday ministries are overshadowing Sundays.** More people participate during the week than on Sundays; people look to their communities for help all week long. Ministry to single adults, chil-

dren and young people—including schools—is widespread. Former "Sunday Schools" frequently are spread out through the week. Retreats become more common.

Effective congregations in the next century—what Easum refers to as "paradigm communities"—will

- have a scriptural focus, but their conservativism will be characterized by a strong "grace" emphasis;
- have evangelism as their dominant agenda, versus the building of local churches;
- emphasize commitment to Christ and each other, rather than membership in a church or a denomination;
- have a passion for excellence in all they do.

Easum concludes with a note of caution: "My largest concern about the future of paradigm communities is that they will never mature to the point of becoming involved in social justice beyond single issue votes such as abortion and homosexuality. Time will tell."[69]

Easum agrees with Mead that the era of Christendom is over, and that mission today and in the future will require a church radically different from what it has been in the recent past. Easum is also very emphatic about the mission of the Church: its job is "to win the world through faith in Christ." Easum sees the equivalent of Mead's "third paradigm" as the rediscovery of "the Apostolic paradigm," applied to the 21st century.

Recognizing the need for innovation and experiment, Easum attempts to identify some tangible new forms that are being developed by people on the "fringe" of the church. Some of those features are already used in Canada by congregations trying to connect with Canadians—notably worship forms, small groups, and lay empowerment. To the extent they prove effective, their use will undoubtedly become more widespread.

HERB MILLER
Vital congregations

Herb Miller is currently the head of the Net Results Resource Center in Lubbock, Texas and recently succeeded Lyle Schaller as Parish Consultant for the Yokefellow Institute. He is regarded as one of North America's top congregational authorities, and is in high demand as speaker and resource person in areas including church growth, evangelism, and leadership development. The material that follows is based on his book, The Vital Congregation, *published by Abingdon Press. (Copyright © 1990. Used by permission.)*

Miller is concerned with seeing that congregations have a vitality that translates into effective ministry. Vital congregations, he says, are congregations that carry out "the ministry of Jesus Christ by saying and doing what Jesus said and did."[70] They help people form connections with God, with each other, and with "great causes"—with God, self, and society.

According to Miller, vital congregations have **ten** dominant characteristics.

1. **Hope**. They have lay and clergy leaders who communicate a vision of hope and expectancy about the future. Hope, says Miller, provides the motivation and energy to develop the other nine vital characteristics. It takes the form of a positive outlook, stimulated by commitment to purpose and faith in the empowerment of God.
2. **Worship.** While churches do many things, their main purpose is helping people connect with God. "Worship" writes Miller, "is the primary way churches accomplish that main thing."[71]
   - Worship should be spiritually and biblically focused, and characterized by warmth, friendliness, enthusiasm, and even humor. There should be variety and innovation within a general format.
   - Worship should be sensitive to the culture of the people present, including having something for people of all ages, including children and young people, and involve them in the services—their presence also encourages parental participation.
   - Music needs to be upbeat and fast moving, yet meet the musical needs of more than one generation and one kind of person.

"Music is 40% of the service," he writes. "Worship and music leaders who insist on serving only one kind of worshiper will, after ten or twenty years, end up with only that kind of person in their services."[72]

3. **Climate.** Vital churches, maintains Miller, create environments that are characterized by love and acceptance. Indications of such a milieu include

- members who make a point of greeting and talking to visitors.
- the way that church personnel speak to people on the phone.
- leaders who are willing to listen to people's problems and ideas.
- acceptance of people whose doctrines and morals are not necessarily ours.
- people having fun.
- emphasis on praising instead of blaming.
- procedures for supporting people during times of stress.
- procedures for contacting people who are absent, including those who are ill, both short-term and long-term.

Miller cites research to show that if people "drop out" for some reason, a visit within six weeks can prevent 85% from becoming inactive; a visit within six months results in about 25% returning to activity; and a visit within a year contributes to about 15% returning.[73] Sometimes there is value in letting a different group start fresh with inactivities. "Some churches have exchanged inactive-member lists with a nearby congregation of their denomination," writes Miller, "and have recovered 30 percent of each other's inactive members by visiting them and inviting them to church."[74]

4. **Involvement.** Leaders of vital congregations, says Miller, know that the more people they involve, the more ministry they will accomplish. Consequently, leaders of such churches delegate responsibilities according to people's gifts.

- Miller makes an important distinction between people **engaged in primary ministry** (the actual work of the church, such as evangelism, pastoral care, teaching, singing, and various other activities and projects) and people who **talk about primary ministry** (e.g., committees). There is a third category of people, says Miller—those who **talk about people who talk about primary ministries** (e.g. boards) and a fourth category who **watch** what everyone is doing. Miller maintains that, because only about 15 to 30% of members typically feel comfortable using verbal skills, it's important to encourage most to **do things** rather than to **discuss things**.

- According to Miller, leaders who expect every member to attend everything that happens in the church are out of touch with times. "In vital, growing congregations of every size," he says, "leaders organize the programing, groups, classes, and activities as a buffet rather than as a one-dish meal. And they refrain from pointing an accusing finger at patrons who refuse to spoon up every dish in the serving line."[75]

5. **Outreach.** Vital congregations reach out beyond their walls and encourage people to connect with Jesus Christ. "Congregational evangelism" has three components:

   a) getting people to attend for the first time,

   b) getting people to return a second and third time, and

   c) getting people involved with Christ and the church.

- One study, Miller points out, shows that about 78% of new church members attend the first time because they are invited by a member.[76] He writes, "As someone has said, 'Shepherds do not beget sheep. Sheep beget sheep.' That process begins through simple invitations to worship."[77]

- People who show up need to be contacted—quickly. If visitors are paid a home visit within 36 hours, 85% will come back next week. The figure drops to 60% for a contact within 72 hours, and 15% if the visit doesn't occur for seven days. The most effective method? Home visits by laypersons. Telephone contacts, Miller adds, reduce the results by at least 75%.

- In time, people need to be invited both to profess Christian faith and join the church.

6. **Assimilation.** People need to be added to the church, and not just to the membership roll, says Miller. Vital congregations, he maintains, adopt attitudes and methods for enthusiastically assimilating new people into church life. Early they are invited to be part of some small church group—a choir, a Sunday school class, a group, a ball team... Within three to six months, they need to be given opportunity to assume some kind of responsibility.

Strategies for facilitating assimilation might also include such practical measures as publishing pictorial directories on a regular basis and making lists of members and their responsibilities available to leaders of congregational groups. People must have a sense of belonging.

7. **Spirituality.** Miller says that vital congregations provide group opportunities for spiritual growth. They include Bible study, prayer, and the chance to relate to like-minded people. The congregational end-in-all is hardly organizational and financial matters. A wide range of small group possibilities are necessary.

8. **Prayer.** Vital congregations adopt attitudes and enact methods that teach members how to nurture prayer. Its importance should be communicated and experienced in worship, in the organizational life of the church, in commitments to pray for each other.

9. **Stewardship.** Vital congregations, says Miller, encourage members to develop sacrificial stewardship of resources—finances, time, and talent. Themes instilled include the importance of giving over receiving, and of giving out of gratitude rather than out of duty. Miller sees people becoming good stewards neither automatically nor naturally, but as a product of preaching, teaching, and stewardship programs.

10. **Service.** Attitudes and methods in vital congregations meet the needs of people in the church, the community, and the world. Ministry to members is important; but also extends outside the church. Such service includes making the church building available to others, encouraging the pastor to service not just the church but the community, and responding to community needs. Service also needs to extend further outward, where congregations are informed about and responsive to national and global matters as well.

Miller offers many insights into some of the main characteristics of healthy congregations in the U.S., Canada, and elsewhere. The kind of churches he writes about are capable not only of serving their own members but also of motivating them to reach out and connect with outsiders, welcoming them and accepting them. Still further, they are congregations that have much to offer—they possess the resources to begin to address newcomers' diverse spiritual, personal, and relational needs. Vital congregations may be somewhat idealized, but to the extent that they can be approximated, they have much to bring to Canadians.

ARNELL MOTZ
A vision for Canada

Since the late 1980s, an effort to engage in more effective evange-
lism in Canada, known as "Vision 2000," has been carried out in
Canada under the auspices of the country's umbrella organization
for evangelicals, the Evangelical Fellowship of Canada. "Vision
2000" is intended to help individual groups find the best methods
of evangelism for their own situations. According to its purpose
statement, "Vision 2000 Canada seeks to serve the Body of Christ
in evangelism so that every person in Canada will have the oppor-
tunity to see, hear and respond to the gospel by the year 2000."
Arnell Motz headed the seven-person research group that attempted
to provide information on the state of the church in Canada and
the needs of the nation. What follows are some of the group's find-
ings, drawn from Motz's edited volume, Reclaiming a Nation, *pub-*
lished in 1990 by the Church Leadership Library in Richmond,
B.C. and used by permission.

According to research group member Murray Moerman, a key to
reaching out to Canadians lies in "planting" new churches. He argues that new churches are required for a number of reasons, including the need
- to keep up with population growth,
- to replace older churches that die,
- to continually create new churches that are energetic, creative,
  and evangelistically effective, and
- to respond to an increasingly diverse Canadian population.

As of the early 1990s, there were just over 23,000 Christian congregations in Canada, with some 40% of these Mainline Protestant, 30% Roman Catholic parishes, and 30% Conservative Protestant congregations.
- This 23,000 total translates into a ratio of just under one congregation for every 1000 people. By comparison, China has some
  43,000 mosques serving approximately 15 million Islamic people, a ratio of one mosque for every 350 Moslems.
- Moerman suggests that the average Canadian congregation can
  minister effectively to fewer than 500 people.

- For Conservative Protestant, to attain one church per 2,000 Canadians by the year 2000, close to 7,000 new churches are required.

Moerman suggests a number of steps to be taken to create "evangelizing churches." He calls for church planting efforts to be grounded in prayer. He stresses the need to analyze the size and makeup of projected populations, as well as carefully to determine appropriate locations. Among the models he offers for church planting are the starting of offspring congregations by "mother" churches, uncovering people through door-to-door surveys, and getting in touch with personal and community needs and responding to them.

Motz himself writes that most Canadian churches have probably seen relatively few outsiders profess Christian faith in recent years. Yet there are some exceptions. The key to reaching people outside the churches, he says, is relationships: "Few come to Christ outside the context of a family or friend."[78] Other effective means of connecting with people who are not involved in the churches include seasonal musicals, teas, breakfasts, topical luncheons, home Bible studies, programs addressing the social needs, and parties and other events aimed at young people. Explicit attempts to minister to immigrants and cultural minorities are also a high priority, and are being carried out fairly extensively.

It's important, says Motz, for congregations not merely to duplicate the activities of others but to respond to the unique callings of their own communities. A key part of such a process is research. Churches have to know their audiences and environments to "contextualize" their ministries. Motz offers guidelines for constructing a community profile that includes objectives, community demographics, social needs, and attitudes toward the church and faith.[79]

He also stresses the importance of clearly understanding one's own congregation. "It can help the leaders understand their people's needs, where they are at in their spiritual lives, and something of their aspirations."[80] He cites the following observation of George Gallup:

...in order to find out what's happening, you need to poll, even every year. What are the priorities? Where do people see improvement made in the church? Is your outreach plan working? Things

like this can be monitored. That's one way to keep on top of events. Often it will take a pastor years to determine the level of knowledge in the parish... Finding this information informally takes time, and you still don't know for sure.[81]

Motz reminds readers that merely gathering information is not enough—it must also be used: "if you are going to ask, you must be prepared to do something as a result." He also stresses that research must be sound research, repeating the adage that "there is only one thing worse than no research and that is bad research."[82] He is emphatic about the importance of research, borrowing these words of church growth expert Peter Wagner:

Theological seminaries need to include...research methodologies in the curricula. If only the current fad of holding nationwide, regional, and even world congresses on evangelism could be harnessed to teach diagnostic skills to church leaders across the board, the cause of evangelism and missions would be advanced in a spectacular way.[83]

Efforts such as "Vision 2000," admits Motz, are not exempt from such a critique. "Our consultations and congresses on evangelism become Christian 'pep rallies' unless, at the heart of their strategies, is research of the 'harvest field' and the 'harvest force.'"[84]

Another group member, Gerald Kraft, argues that to reach today's generation the church needs to be sensitized to the needs in our communities and nation. While each church is limited in what it can do, each congregation can do something. According to Kraft, the primary areas of need include ministry to single parents, previously-married and never-married singles; couples living together; street kids; ex-convicts; people suffering from AIDS; prostitutes; alcoholics and drug abusers; persons living in poverty; people with cancer; handicapped and disabled persons; those who are depressed; and the victims of sexual abuse. Christians, he says, must aspire to be like Jesus—not only **speaking** about compassion but also **exhibiting** it, to the point that "our compassion is so transparent" that such outsiders "will reach out to us."[85]

Motz points out that outreach in the '90s needs to be built on a relational model. It also will involve "going out to where society is and where society hurts."[86] Change and renewal is required in a number of areas, he says, such as increased prayer, commitment to evangelism, fostering discipleship, being willing to change, exemplifying compassion and integrity, and being committed to working together.

The "Vision 2000" research reminds us that efforts to connect with Canadians will require the establishing of new congregations, as well as attracting people to existing churches that are creative and innovative in responding to the needs of the people around them. Motz and his associates underline the key role that relationships play, both in retaining existing members and in reaching out to outsiders. They further emphasize the importance of sound research, not only so that congregations can get a clear reading of the milieus in which they attempt to minister, but also in order that congregations might more clearly understand themselves.

LEITH ANDERSON
A vision for the next century

Leith Anderson is the senior pastor of Wooddale Church in suburban Minneapolis, a congregation that he has helped guide through change and growth. Wooddale has been particularly successful in both meeting the spiritual needs of its people and reaching out to its surrounding community. The following material is drawn from his book, A Church for the 21st Century, *published by Bethany House Publishers, 11300 Hampshire Ave. S., Minneapolis, MN 55438. (Copyright © 1992. Used by permission.)*

Anderson sees the dawning of the 21st century being accompanied by worldwide spiritual interest that crosses religious, political, and cultural lines. The situation represents an extraordinary opportunity. But typically, it is being greeted more with fear than with fascination. The churches that will flourish, he says, will be those that "talk about and offer authentic supernatural experiences" and offer answers "from the authority of the Bible and a Christian world view."[87]

Changes have begun to take place, writes Anderson, with the new shapes and forms of the church including these:

- **megachurches** with 2,000-plus worshipers that function like large shopping malls offering a broad array of services;
- **metachurches** based on a large number of lay-led small groups that meet for worship services but accomplish most of their ministry through the group gatherings;
- **seven-days-a-week churches** where emphasis is placed on activities and groups that meet whenever is best for those involved— including varied times for worship services;
- **house churches** that involve small gatherings of people in homes that cater to family relationships or special interests;
- **TV churches** which may, with the advent of interactive television, become an increasing reality in the next century;
- **Wal-Mart churches** that particularly serve regional rural markets, and emphasize friendliness and programs, that are customer-driven, and that retain the traditions of small communities;
- **new churches** where flexibility, openness to newcomers, outreach, and general innovation are possible, especially for the first ten

years or so of their existence;
- **traditional churches** that have particular appeal to those who are reacting to change, do not want to lose control, are worried about the future, and are attracted to the durability and credibility associated with the past.

In Anderson's mind, the new leaders for a new century will be people who are attuned to their culture, are good communicators, have an entrepreneurial spirit and are risk takers, and are godly people. Unrealistic expectations, dysfunctional churches, personal problems, and inadequate training, all add up to stress—as does the seemingly enviable trait of success, in the form of "encore anxiety" about trying to sustain and repeat accomplishments.

But Anderson adds, "by no means do all pastors currently fail." In the U.S., he reminds his readers, "there are over 300,000 serving parishes, and most don't quit, are not fired, and probably don't consider themselves to be failures."[88] It's just that change is making things increasingly difficult for many people in paid ministry.

The current concern about leadership, says Anderson, sometimes fails to give adequate attention to the importance of "followership": "It should surprise us that so much is said about leaders and so little about followers, especially among Christians committed to the Bible. The Bible says comparatively little about leadership and a great deal about followership."[89] "Not everyone can be a leader. It takes only a few leaders to fulfill God's goals. But it takes many followers."[90]

For Anderson, the kind of followers needed by the church will be characterized by these four factors:
- **wisdom**—they know **who** to follow;
- **priorities**—they recognize that the church "can't afford the luxury of petty differences and individual preferences" and are "willing to set aside their personal priorities and align with the great priorities of the body";[91]
- **loyalty**—they have staying power in the face of criticism and negativism;
- **support**—they work together with leaders, are accountable, and expect the same of their leaders.

According to Anderson, churches that focus on others ("outward churches") rather than on themselves ("inward churches") will encounter a number of hurdles. Even when they are committed to ensuring that people already in the church are not neglected, issues will arise over the pastor's time, finances, assimilating newcomers, and a wide array of structural changes ranging from new activities to changing the name of the church.

Drawing on other experts, Anderson suggests tangible ways of "connecting" with people outside the congregation. These include making contact with newcomers on moving day, attending garage sales and yard sales, and involvement in community organizations and activities, sports, and block parties.

As to where to actually begin at the congregational level, Anderson offers ministers the following steps:
- pray for wisdom and direction; add others, and become a prayer group;
- specify privately what you want to see happen and how long you are willing to stick with the church;
- talk to church leaders, asking them to join with you in exploring possibilities concerning the church's future;
- diagnose your situation with your leaders and possibly with trusted outsiders, describing what your church is and should become;
- prescribe what needs to be done, keeping the list short and beginning with simple things that are likely to work;
- broaden the effort, having church leaders spread the word about what the church is going to do;
- review and recycle, repeating and extending the process: "In many ways it is more important to be moving in the right direction than worrying about how fast you are progressing."[92]

Anderson is helpful in identifying a variety of possible forms and shapes that 21st century congregations might take. He also reminds us of some of the obstacles facing people in leadership positions, while drawing attention to the often overlooked importance of "followers." His guidelines for getting started further represent his commitment to ensuring that concrete ministry takes place.

GEORGE BARNA
Marketing and more

*Since the mid-1980s, George Barna has made a concerted effort
to provide American churches with information and marketing expertise in order to help them carry out more effective ministry. He
is the founder and president of the California-based marketing
research company, Barna Research Group, and the author of a
number of best-selling books. The material that follows is drawn
from two of his books,* Marketing the Church *(adapted from* Marketing the Church *by George Barna. Copyright © 1988 by
NavPress. Used by permission of NavPress, Colorado Springs, CO.
All rights reserved. For copies call 1-800-366-7788) and* User
Friendly Churches *(Copyright © 1991, Regal Books, Ventura, CA
93003. Used by permission.)*

According to Barna, churches engaging in ministry today need to
recognize that they are in a business—"the business of ministry."
They consequently need to "be run with the same wisdom and
savvy that characterizes any for-profit business."[93]

In today's world, that also means that marketing needs to be
an essential component of churches—as indispensable as it is to
successful companies. He doesn't mince his words: "My concen-
tration... is that the major problem plaguing the Church is its failure to embrace a marketing orientation in what has become a mar-
keting-driven environment."[94] He continues, "I believe that developing a marketing orientation is precisely what the Church needs
to do if we are to make a difference in the spiritual health of this
nation."[95] The Church won't totally collapse if it fails to embrace
such an orientation, he says, but it will not able to take advantage
of current opportunities for outreach and growth.

Barna readily acknowledges that many people have difficulty
with the idea of applying marketing concepts to religious groups
and ministry. In fact, he goes into considerable detail trying to
show his critics why such apprehension is unwarranted.[96] Nonetheless, he argues that such a model can be used with integrity.
Church leaders already refer to "church growth strategies," "bridge
building," "outreach," and "promotion" to describe some of the

activities he has in mind. "However," he says almost defiantly, "I call these activities **marketing**."[97] That's what they are called outside of religious communities—to the point that people in the business world, for example, seem dismayed that such thinking should sound either novel or inappropriate to religious leaders.

The Church, he argues, exists in a competitive environment: "The real competition is not with other churches—it is with organizations, opportunities, and philosophies that provide people with an alternative to the Christian life." More specifically, he says, "Our main competition is from organizations like ABC, CBS, Universal Studios, MGM, K-Mart, 7-Eleven, JC Penney, and so forth." And, he adds, "organizations like these are highly sophisticated marketers!"[98]

Marketing concepts, writes Barna, can be restructured to address the needs and purposes of the church. According to marketing literature, successful marketing experiences result from achieving a balance between the famous "Four P's"—**product, place, promotion, and price**. In churches, he says,
- the **product** is relationships, with Christ and others;
- the **place** is flexible—reaching out and touching people does not have any geographic or physical boundaries;
- the key to **promotion** is personal recommendation, through establishing and nurturing relationships with other people;
- **price** is the cost of commitment to the product.

Appropriate balance between the "Four P's" depends on a fairly orderly process: **research, vision, production, marketing plan, implementation, and feedback.**

Barna argues that churches—just like well-run businesses—need to engage in **research** to determine personal and community needs and interests. While a well-focused **vision** is rare among churches, he says, it nonetheless is essential. Churches have to know where they are, where they're going, and how they are going to get there. They need to develop explicit **marketing plans** that specify the strategies and "tactics" which are necessary to reach their objectives—keeping in mind human and financial resources. (Barna differentiates between "strategies" as related to vision, and "tactics" as being "the things you do to fulfill your strategies."[99])

Implementation has to be planned, overseen, and monitored. **Feedback** must be constantly obtained to evaluate the effectiveness of what is being attempted.

On the subject of reaching out to outsiders specifically, Barna asserts that some traditional "tactics" should be avoided; others should be attempted only with caution; still others, he asserts, "work."

- Three traditional tactics that have little or no value in marketing a church today are home visitation, "passive media" (such as a sign on a church lawn), and paid mass media advertising.
- High risk tactics, where people can "win big or lose big," include media ministry, organizing community events, direct mailings, and telemarketing. The latter, for example, "is plagued," says Barna, "by the same weakness as door-to-door visitation—there is no [personal]_relationship on which credibility is based."[100]
- Three tactics that work are
  1. **Personal Invitation**, reflecting the research that the second most important reason why people attend their current church—after *legacy*—is *relational* in the form of an invitation from someone.
  2. **Small group studies**, usually held in homes and focusing on the Bible, spirituality, and/or other topics of interest. Again, relationship-building is key.
  3. **Program**, where emphasis is given to meeting needs, such as providing instruction and activities for children.

Numbers, Barna insists, are not everything. Yet, he says, "I believe there is an indivisible relationship between quality and quantity when it comes to church growth... The more successful a church is at fulfilling people's needs, the greater are its chances for growth."[101]

Barna maintains that a dominant characteristic of churches that are in touch with people is that they are "user friendly."

Just as a well-designed computer system enables even computer novices to use it effectively, user friendly churches enable a broad spectrum of people to come to know and serve the living God. ...[They are not] user friendly in the sense of compromising this gospel of the historic faith of the church just to make friends with the age. Each of these churches affirms the gospel of Christ boldly and without apology. But they are equally firm in their intent to

*listen to the audiences they target, and to meet contemporary felt
needs as the gospel directs.*[102]

Barna stresses that every church is faced with a unique set of circumstances. Therefore congregations are seldom successful when
they simply try to copy models—such as Willow Creek—that have
worked elsewhere. Yet, he says, there are "a series of church growth
principles that are working today and can be adapted to your situation."[103] They include the following.

1. **Positive attitude**. Pro-ministry, enthusiastic, we-can-do-it out-
    look. An expression of the perspectives of the leaders within the
    church. Cultivation of lively context, excitement about ministry.
2. **People-oriented**. Focus is not programs but people and their
    needs. Sometimes programs are appropriate, sometimes not. Em-
    phasis on outreach to others versus inreach: "Less self-absorp-
    tion, they found, leads to a healthier perspective about the sig-
    nificance and severity of one's own dilemmas."[104]
3. **Recognized limits.** Do not try to do everything. Focus on vision
    for ministry and commitment to quality. Expand to new areas of
    ministry as resources permit. Accept that whatever you do, you
    will not attract everyone.
4. **Quality.** Ministry is characterized by integrity, excellence, con-
    sistency, and reliability. Churches are open to feedback.
5. **Strong leadership**. Pastors for growing churches value ministry
    over structure, can delegate, have social skills, can make deci-
    sions, are visible, are accountable.
6. **Strong laity.** Being part of the church is more than merely at-
    tending; people are active participants in the church's ministry.
    They are encouraged to identify their gifts, refine them, and en-
    gage in significant tasks while being supported by the church.
    Talents are matched with tasks.
7. **Prayer.** People view prayer as a foundation stone of ministry.
    They consistently include prayer in their services, events, meet-
    ings, and personal ministries.
8. **Relational links.** People consciously invite other people to at-
    tend church. They also take responsibility for on-site hospitality
    and post-visit debriefing.
9. **Youth ministry**. Churches attempt to identify and address the
    needs of children and youth. Flexibility, games, fun, relation-
    ships, music, videos, and energy are all part of the mix. Youth

expect excellence from the church and are unwilling to accept mediocrity.

10. **Outreach-oriented.** Ministry is oriented to addressing not only the needs of those involved but also the varied spiritual, relational, physical, and emotional needs of other people. "Churches," Barna says, "usually die from the inside out. Death is largely due to an inward focus, rather than an outward concern."[105]

Barna concludes, "The time is ripe for new models of ministry to be tried, tested, refined and disseminated. The time is ripe for a new generation of church leaders to emerge, anxious to lead the Church into an age of growth and impact."[106]

For too long, church leaders and others have been inclined to view churches as organizationally unique—somehow exempt from the strengths and vulnerabilities of other organizations. Barna brings a stinging critique to such thinking, in calling churches to recognize that they are organizations, and to function as efficiently as possible in connecting with outsiders. But he does more. He attempts to show churches how it can be done, both by offering theory about marketing, and by sketching the characteristics of churches who are successfully employing such strategies.

LYLE E. SCHALLER
Getting innovative

Perhaps no one has played a more dominant and prominent role in working with American religious groups in the last half of this century than Lyle Schaller. Widely regarded as the leading authority on congregational life, he has provided consultation to groups from more than 70 religious traditions. Schaller is the author of some 40 books and the editor of over 40 more. The ideas that follow are drawn from his 1994 book, Innovations in Ministry: Models for the 21st Century. *(Copyright © 1994 by Abingdon Press. Used by permission.)*

According to Schaller, the most exciting era in the history of American Protestantism was perhaps the early 19th century—complete with the emergence of the Methodists and Baptists, the Second Great Awakening, the challenge of foreign missionaries, the founding of the first theological seminaries, and the birth of a range of nondenominational agencies.

American Protestantism's second most exciting era in history, says Schaller, has been the last quarter of—yes—this 20th century. He sees the period as a time characterized by great "openness to new forms of ministry, the birth of a new expression of the faith through music, a more sophisticated use of television to communicate the gospel, and the emergence of new forms of interchurch cooperation."[107]

Consumerism, he writes, has forced churches to be more sensitive to the religious needs of people. They have responded, he claims, by creating new forms of ministry that have led, not to a decrease, but to an **increase** in the total numbers of people who are worshiping in the U.S. churches. "The vitality, relevance, and sensitivity of ministry in most of today's Protestant congregations," he writes, "is impressive!" Schaller is quick to offer this important qualification: "Such a positive diagnosis cannot be offered about the state of every congregation... American Catholicism is facing unprecedented problems. Likewise, several Protestant denominational systems are overdue for reform, and some will survive only if they are reformed."

Still, he argues, all things considered, "The good news greatly exceeds the bad news about the current state of American Protestantism."[108]

Schaller says that the problems of some groups have created opportunity for other groups. In this, he reflects the thinking of U.S. sociologists Roger Finke and Rodney Stark[109] who argue that, throughout American history, the ongoing need for spirituality has resulted in a pattern of some groups declining and other groups quickly moving in to increase their "market shares." Mainstream denominational cutbacks, for example, created a vacuum that others quickly moved to fill, including large numbers of independent and frequently charismatic congregations.

"The decision by any one congregation or denomination 'not to do that'," writes Schaller, "does not mean it will not happen. Someone will come along to fill that vacuum."[110] New and often highly innovative ministries have been launched to respond to personal needs and the demand for better quality. In some churches, the results include the following.

- Sizable numbers of baby boomers can be found, particularly in new, large, regional congregations that focus on the personal and religious needs of people rather than on the institutional agendas of churches and denominations.
- Worship is fast-paced and emphasizes preaching, teaching, and a wave of creative new music and drama.
- Worship and study are spread throughout the week.
- There is a greater emphasis on grace, love, and hope, and a reduced emphasis on guilt and fear.
- Mission increasingly is being done "at home" in the congregations' local communities, with mission defined in terms of the total health of individuals.
- Congregations and ministries are becoming more varied, socially, economically, ethnically, and racially.
- Interchurch cooperation has grown considerably, more by the efforts of congregations and pastors than of denominational offices.
- Central city ministries are probably healthier than ever.

Such developments, says Schaller, reflect the emergence of a new model for ministry. "For generations the organizational self-image of a Protestant congregation in the United States was a gathered community with its own private meeting place and served by a pastor and perhaps other paid staff as well as volunteer leaders. Its ministry was pointed to with pride as an in-house affair." The assumption was that ministry depended on people "coming to our meeting place."

The new model, Schaller says, "moves the congregation and its ministries away from the controlling center and toward the collaborating perimeter. The model is less protectionist and more dangerous."[111]

At the heart of this new model for ministry is the idea that the most productive strategy "begins with going to the people, meeting them on their turf, and beginning with their agenda." Schaller adds, "That is *not* a new idea. The best model can be found in the New Testament in the ministries of Jesus, Paul and others."[112]

Schaller maintains that if congregations respond to people's religious needs with sensitivity and care, people will want to be part of those congregations. Well-known "success story" congregations (such as the Willow Creek Community Church in Illinois, the Brunswick Reformed Church in Ohio, and the Saddleback Community Church in southern California) have at least two key qualities in common, he says:

1. they define their audiences with precision
2. they have clarity about the nature of their mission.

Given the resource problems of many denominations and the growing emphasis on local mission, says Schaller, the initiative for new ventures in ministry increasingly may come from large, regional congregations—what he calls "Key Churches." Such ventures also can be expected to see greater participation of trained laity. In Schaller's words, "lay volunteers, not money, are the crucial resource in implementing new strategies for outreach. Instead of doing ministry, the clergy are being asked to identify, enlist, nurture, disciple, train, place, support and resource teams of lay volunteers who will do the work."[113]

Key churches, a lay work force, and **"off-campus" ministries** are the three central components in what Schaller sees as ministries of the future.

A "Key Church Strategy" involves establishing a number of

indigenous satellite churches or ministries from a strong, "Key Church" base. Examples include immigrant missions, house churches, and multihousing missions—forms that might evolve into autonomous worshiping communities. Other possible settings for mission ministry include nursing homes, prisons, and hospitals, and schools. Many of these ministries, says Schaller, will be short-lived; some (such as programs for children or parents) may last only months or even weeks. This strategy, in his mind, assumes that the "delivery of social services and the role of advocate is always accompanied by the gospel."[114]

Off-campus ministries, that have as their long-term goal the creation of autonomous worshiping communities, can take at least three main forms, says Schaller.

1. **New ministries**. One venue is apartments, where Key Church volunteers establish rapport with a manager and set out to respond to the varied needs and interests of residents (e.g. English as a second language, children, single-parents, desire for social activities). In time, when "the right to be heard has been earned," the program can be expanded to include Bible study and Sunday school classes, perhaps even a worship service. Other possible locations might be a student dormitory, a high school... Objectives include creating a comfortable setting, responding to people who have common characteristics,[115] and focusing on the agenda of the people to be served.

2. **Assisting "wounded birds."** Here, a strong Key Church functions as a "sponsoring" congregation that essentially "adopts" declining congregations no longer able to sustain viable ministries in their neighborhoods or regions. The sponsoring church has as its central goal the reaching and serving of new constituencies and new generations of people. Ideally, the "wounded bird" is an asset to the sponsoring church, providing a new opportunity for ministry. Schaller emphasizes that "the goal is not to enable that wounded bird to fly back into yesterday, but rather to help it become a resource for a new tomorrow." With a new constituency and a new role: "that wounded bird can fly again, but it won't be the same old bird, and it may fly higher and farther, as well as in a new direction."[116]

3. **The multisite option**. A full schedule of programing is offered at

the old site with a duplicate schedule offered at a second site. The benefits include exploring a new site without abandoning the old, the possibility of reaching and serving additional people, the opportunity to explore alternative types of worship and ministry, and the maintaining of full human and financial resources, rather than dividing them in the course of trying to establish a new congregation. One board, one budget, one staff, one senior minister are involved. Neither site is treated as "second-class."

Schaller does not suggest that the "Key Church strategy" will be—or even should be—widely adapted. He estimates that perhaps one in fifty congregations might be willing and able to become a part of such a strategy. Yet such a level of involvement, he suggests, could dramatically increase the amount of new outreach ministries launched in any conference, association, synod, diocese, or region in any one year.[117]

Schaller reminds us that the receptivity and needs of people signal the opportunity for ministry. In the midst of the problems being experienced by mainline American Protestantism, there are signs of vitality. Not all congregations are failing. On the contrary, the problems of some groups have actually created an opportunity for others. Good numbers of congregations are engaging in new and highly innovative forms of ministry, and are experiencing considerable success. Even in Canada where "the religious market" is far less lively—in part because denominational ties continue to be deeply ingrained—it is clear that some groups are succeeding in ministering to a wide cross-section of Canadians. Like their U.S. counterparts, they seem to be in touch with their audiences and are ministering to their diverse spiritual, personal, and relational needs. Schaller's call to go out and minister to people on "their own turf" through new venues, old venues, and multisites is one that needs to be taken seriously in this country, if "connection" is to become a reality.

Conclusion

Recently, an active Roman Catholic layman who is familiar with both *Unknown Gods* and many of the ideas in this book said to me, "There's one gnawing question that I still have. What's the point of it all? Why do you want to see churches rejuvenated?"

It's an mportant question, one that takes me back to where I began. Disappointing though it may be for some people to hear it, I again emphasize that my goal is not merely to help rejuvenate churches. **My goal is to help churches engage in improved ministry—because large numbers of Canadians need what the churches potentially have to give.**

In my mind, the real tragedy about declining participation is not the sight of empty pews. It's the fact that such a situation means the spiritual, personal, and social needs of large numbers of Canadians are going unmet.

The point is not church growth; the point is ministry.

Does growth equal evangelism?

For all the good things the church growth literature may offer, much of what is written comes precariously close to magnifying numbers as ends in themselves.

Well-known church growth proponent Peter Wagner, for example, concludes his widely-read book, *Your Church Can Grow*, with a chapter entitled, "God Wants Your Church to Grow!" Wagner sees numerical expansion as directly related to churches fulfilling the Great Commission and "making disciples." Growth presumably will be a reflection of outreach.

Maybe—and maybe not. I learned a long time ago that there can be growth without much evangelism, and evangelism without much growth. Other rather prosaic factors, such as the recruitment of geographically-mobile members and the addition of members' children, can have a far greater impact on the population sizes of groups. Wagner is also well aware of such realities.

Does evangelism equal ministry?

Further, while evangelism may mean that spiritual needs are being met, it does not necessarily mean that ministry to people is complete. On the contrary, individuals still have personal and social needs that have to be addressed.

"Leading people to Christ" also does not mean that churches can turn a blind eye to the social and cultural conditions that shape people's lives, and that sometimes have to be altered. It's sad commentary that Peter Wagner finds himself reminding growth-minded churches, "To the degree that socially involved churches become engaged in social action, as distinguished from social services, they can expect church growth to diminish.[118]

The fact is, ministry is not carried out in response to what the polls say is safe turf. Churches sometimes have to take social and cultural chances in the name of ministry. In doing so, they are only being true to the Christian tradition, beginning with Jesus, the disciples, and Paul.

And that is not always popular. There are still many churches—and many within those churches—that equate Christian faith with withdrawal from worldly concerns. In 1994, Bert Witvoet, the editor of the independent Christian Reformed newspaper, *Christian Courier*, wrote an editorial criticizing "the tendency among North American Christians to reduce Christianity to a personal relationship with God." When the *London Free Press* reprinted his editorial, Witvoet received a number of letters that, he says, "confirmed my worst suspicions." He quotes one of them:

> *The whole book [that is, the Bible] is written concerning only two things, and they are Christ and the church... Leave economics, legal ethics, city landscaping, politics, sports, music, and commerce to lobby groups. Let us render the things that are Caesar's to Caesar, and the things that are God's to God."*[119]

Does growth equal ministry?

Which leads us to another key question: are growing churches necessarily engaging in effective ministry? In the midst of general concern about numerical decline, we hear a growing number of stories about congregations growing spectacularly.[120]

- The Yoido Full Gospel Church in Seoul, Korea has become the largest congregation in the world. It has some 500,000 members who meet in cell groups through the week and gather together on the weekend for multiple services in a 10,000 seat sanctuary.
- The Young Nak Presbyterian Church in the same city has a 20,000 seat facility and some 75,000 members.
- In Santiago, Chile, the Jotabeche Methodist Pentecostal Church allows its 100,000 members to attend services only one Sunday night each month, because it has seating for only 16,000; other Sundays they worship in 40 satellite churches around the city.
- The largest U.S. church appears to be the First Baptist Church in Hammond, Indiana, with a total membership of about 80,000 and a weekly attendance of over 20,000. Highland Baptist in Chattanooga, Tennessee has some 60,000 members, First Baptist Dallas around 25,000.
- Willow Creek Community Church, some 30 miles from Chicago in South Barrington, Illinois, has a weekly attendance of over 14,000 and a $15 million facility. Its ministry is geared to Baby Boomers where "seeker services" are held on weekends. Services for believers happen mid-week. Small groups are an integral part of the church's ministry.
- The New Hope Community Church in Portland, Oregon has some 5,000 members who gather on Sundays for services at a 3,000 seat facility. Responding to Robert Schuller's challenge to "Find a need and fill it, find a hurt and heal it," the founding pastor, Dale Galloway, has encouraged the forming of 500 small groups ("TLC" or "Tender Loving Care" groups) that meet across the city during the week, directed by trained lay pastors. The strategy of this "side-door-evangelism" effort involves, successively, a tie to a Christian, a tie to the church, and a tie to Christ.[121]

Canada does not have anywhere near the American number of mega-churches. Yet, "success stories" nonetheless are being told. By way of illustration, the charismatic, non-denominational publication, *Dominion Magazine*, reported the following in its inaugural issue in the summer of 1993.[122]

- Eglise Vie et Réveil in Montreal was established in 1974. Some 1,600 people attend the church's four Sunday services. It has over 1,000 cell groups and a television ministry.

- The Windsor Christian Fellowship was founded in 1982. More than 1,000 people attend its two Sunday services. It has a Bible college and a specific ministry to people in nursing homes as well as the homeless.
- The Word of Life Centre of Red Deer, Alberta is less that 25 years old. It attracts 800 people to its two Sunday Services, has established a Bible college and attempts to address drug and moral issues of high school youth.
- The Word of Life Church in St. Catharines was founded in 1990. Already it has some 1,200 people attending two Sunday services, home groups, a Bible school, and a nationwide television ministry.

The message usually implied in such accounts is that by taking a close look at what these churches have done and extracting some basic principles, "your church" can grow too. American church growth proponent Elmer Towns writes, in a matter-of-fact manner, that growing and innovative churches "understand marketing. In short, they not only can preach, teach, counsel and evangelize; they can run a church like a business." He adds, "The Church of the future will be more influenced by business methods than ever before, rather than following traditional ecclesiastical styles of operation."[123]

Not everyone is equally excited about the success stories of the megachurches.
- Douglas Webster, a Presbyterian teacher and pastor in Colorado, recently published a book entitled, *Selling Jesus: What's Wrong With Marketing the Church.* Some of his concerns can be chalked up to a reaction to the marketing model, rather than to the ideas involved. Still, Webster objects that the goal of the church is not merely to attract more and more people to Jesus. Referring to Willow Creek's effort to reach Baby Boomer prototype "unchurched Harry," Webster writes, "If 'unchurched Harry' feels perfectly at home in our churches, then chances are that we have no longer an authentic household of faith, but a popular cultural religion."[124]
- The Duke Divinity School duo of Stanley Hauerwas and William Willimon maintain that, rather than being societally-encompassing, the church today is best viewed as a colony where Christians

are "resident aliens." "We believe that things have changed for the church residing in America," they say, "and that faithfulness to Christ demands that we either change or else go the way of all compromised forms of the Christian faith."[125]

- And evangelical sociologist Tony Campolo writes that the prophets would not have much patience with today's superchurches. "They would claim that such churches only help people to become better adjusted to our consumer-oriented society," he says, "instead of calling them to reject it."[126]

The debate about the virtues and vices of superchurches can go on forever. What does seem indisputable, however, is that **growth as such is not synonymous with ministry.** To simply find ways of getting churches to grow is to miss the point of why growth should be taking place.

Growth as an outcome of ministry

I think that the ministry of Jesus suggests a solution to the controversy about numbers and integrity of ministry. What he did and how people responded suggest that numbers and integrity are not polar opposites.

As Jesus moved among the people of his time, he obviously experienced diverse responses. Yet, as he ministered to the varied needs of the women, men, and children he encountered, "multitudes," we are told, followed him. Of course he experienced opposition, indifference, and hostility. Still, to the extent that his message and ministry hit a responsive chord, people followed him. His ministry was not about growth; but growth was an outcome of his ministry.

I have been reminding people for some time now[127] that we give our lives—our time, our money, our energy—to those things that we see as significant. To the extent that people find significance in churches—that is, to the extent that the churches touch their lives by responding to their fundamental spiritual, personal, and social needs—there is every reason to believe that many will want to be part of those churches.

No, I'm not suggesting that churches should only locate affiliates, determine their needs, and "service" people. I believe that the Christian message also calls for a response in personal commitment—Jesus is still asking men, women, and children to follow him. Affiliates should be ministered to, but with the expectation that they, in turn, will share in the church's task of ministering to others. Two examples:

- An LDS friend told me about a woman whose husband had left her. She had three young children to support and, at the time of the separation, was not employed. "We have given her food for three months," he said. "But we have also conveyed to her that we need her help in our ministry to others. She happily agreed, and has been helping us with church mailings from her home."
- Bill Hybels says that at Willow Creek, relationships lead to contact with the church, hopefully to profession of Christian faith, followed in turn by service. The church's "network ministry" helps people to discover their spiritual gifts and direct them to appropriate opportunities for service.[128]

In sum, churches need to determine Canadians' spiritual, personal, and social needs, and respond to those needs, **with the clear expectation that people who are ministered to will in turn share in efforts to minister to others**.

The result will be numerical growth, grounded not in the pursuit of single-dimensional evangelism or the desire to simply put people in pews. The result will be growth as a natural outcome of meaningful ministry.

There's got to be more!

"There's got to be more!" are the words being spoken by significant numbers of people outside of Canada's churches who are looking for more fulfilling lives. It's also a phrase that comes out of the mouths of exasperated church leaders, who look at declining attendances and wonder what the future holds.

If the number of people requiring ministry is increasing, then this is anything but a time for churches to be rejoicing in declining numbers. This is a time to respond, and to say with determination, "There's got to be more!"

During a time in prison, the Apostle Paul wrote these words: "We are perplexed, but not unto despair."

These are days characterized by considerable confusion concerning ministry. Many who value faith are perplexed. But, like the Apostle, there is no need for despair. There is, however, a great need to respond.

Endnotes

1 Funding has been provided by the CBC, the federal Solicitor General's office, the United Church, and The University of Lethbridge (1975), the Social Sciences and Humanities Research Council (1980, 1985), the federal Social Trends Directorate (1984), the Lilly Endowment (1990, 1995), and Lilly's Louisville Institute for the Study of Protestantism and American Culture (1992).

2 The five books are *The Emerging Generation,* 1985; *Fragmented Gods,* 1987; *Mosaic Madness,* 1990; *Teen Trends,* 1992; and *Unknown Gods,* 1993. Most of the articles are listed in the reference sections of these books.

3 See *Fragmented Gods,* 1987:214-227.

4 I was amused, after penning this line, to find that George Barna used the same phrase in wrapping up his *User Friendly Churches* (1991:191). I just wanted you to know that this is sheer coincidence of thought, not plagiarism!

5 Ward, 1994:96-97.

6 Bellah et al. 1985

7 See, for example, Nash and Berger, 1962; Parsons, 1963; Kotre, 1971; Caplovitz and Sherrow, 1977; Hunsberger, 1983; Kirkpatrick and Shaver, 1990; Bibby and Posterski, 1992.

8 See, for example, Bibby and Brinkerhoff 1994.

9 See Bibby 1994:16.

10 See, for example, Roozen, McKinney, and Thompson 1990; Roof 1993; Bibby 1993:12-22.

11 See, for example, Mauss, 1969; Hunsberger, 1980; Ozorak, 1989; Hoge, Johnson, and Luidens, 1993:243.

12 Cited in *Fragmented Gods 1987:5.*

13 See, for example, Barna 1991; Anderson 1991; Schaller 1994; Posterski and Barker 1993:53.

14 Hoge, Johnson, and Luidens, 1994.

15 Hadaway and Marler 1993:97

16 Roof and McKinney 1987:167.

17 Posterski and Barker 1993:53-54.

18 Bibby 1993:33-36.

19 Hoge, Johnson, and Luidens 1994:120.

20 Bibby and Posterski, 1992:53.

21 *Maclean's,* October 10, 1994.

22 Roxburgh, 1993:125-126.

23 Includes "North American."

24 Russell 1993:176

25 Muriel Duncan, *United Church Observer,* November, 1993:8.

26 Based on Bibby, 1993:173.

27 See, for example, Berger, 1961.

28 Cited in Towns 1990:57

29 Bibby, 1987:271.

30 I am indebted to "Bud" Phillips of Vancouver School of Theology for reflections that have contributed to this chapter.

31 Fraser, 1993:46-47.

32 My managing editor, Jim Taylor, offers this interesting observation: "Personally, I suspect that altruism is just egoism applied to a larger kin-group—that is, caring for the welfare of all like-minded people (or causes) rather than only for the individual." He also told me to ignore the comment...

33 Freud, 1962.

34 See Proverbs 22.6.

35 Schaller 1994:39

36 See, for example, Roof, 1993; Roozen, McKinney, and Thomp-

son, 1990
[37] See, for example, Bibby and Posterski, *The Emerging Generation,* 1985:196-197; Bibby and Posterski, *Teen Trends,* 1992:186-194.
[38] Bibby 1994. Incidentally, the attendance difference between those who moved and those who didn't persisted even when other factors such as age, employment status, and distance of the move, were taken into account.
[39] Cited in Bibby, 1987:30.
[40] Luke 15:3-4,8; NIV.
[41] Posterski and Bibby, 1988:48.
[42] See, for example, Hadaway, 1990; Marler and Hadaway, 1993.
[43] See *Unknown Gods*, 1993:260-261.
[44] Slightly modified with permission from Stiller, 1991:12,15-16.
[45] Bibby, 1993:221-222.
[46] Dudley, 1983:xi.
[47] Drawn from Kawano, 1992:63-64,70,44.
[48] Mead, 1991:v.
[49] Mead, 1991:v.
[50] Mead, 1991:6.
[51] Mead, 1991:43.
[52] Mead, 1991:58.
[53] Mead, 1991:58.
[54] Mead, 1991:67.
[55] Mead, 1991:73.
[56] Mead, 1991:vi.
[57] Mead, 1991:87.
[58] Mead 1994:x.
[59] Mead 1994:31
[60] Mead, 1994:31.
[61] Mead 1994:115-117
[62] Mead 1994:120
[63] Easum, 1993:15.
[64] Easum, 1993:12.
[65] Easum, 1993:13.
[66] Easum, 1993:19.
[67] Easum, 1993:56.
[68] Easum, 1993:20.
[69] Easum, 1993:112.
[70] Miller, 1990:16.
[71] Miller, 1990:28.
[72] Miller, 1990:34,36.
[73] Miller, 1990:53.
[74] Miller, 1990:54.
[75] Miller, 1990:67.
[76] Miller, 1990:78.
[77] Miller, 1993:79.
[78] Motz, 1990:143.
[79] For specific help in putting together such a profile, see Motz, 1990:191-205
[80] Motz, 1990:205.
[81] Cited in Motz, 1990:205-206.
[82] Motz, 1990:207. Motz also offers readers a detailed example of a ministry assessment questionnaire on pages 208 212.
[83] Cited in Motz, 1990:213.
[84] Motz, 1991:213.
[85] Motz, 1990:238.
[86] Motz, 1990: 249.
[87] Anderson, 1992:22,24.
[88] Anderson, 1992:80.
[89] Anderson, 1992:222.
[90] Anderson, 1992:224.
[91] Anderson, 1992:226.
[92] Anderson, 1992:246.
[93] Barna, 1988:26.
[94] Barna, 1988:23.
[95] Barna, 1988:12.
[96] See, for example, Barna, 1988:1-19,29-37.
[97] Barna, 1988:13.
[98] Barna, 1988:28.
[99] Barna, 1988:107.
[100] Barna, 1988:114.
[101] Barna, 1988:17.
[102] Barna, 1991:16
[103] Barna, 1991:20.
[104] Barna, 1991:47.
[105] Barna, 1991:110.
[106] Barna, 1991:191.
[107] Schaller, 1994:12.
[108] Schaller, 1994:15.
[109] Finke and Stark, 1991
[110] Schaller, 1994:45.

[111] Schaller, 1994:29.

[112] Schaller, 1994:89.

[113] Schaller, 1994:60.

[114] Schaller, 1994:76.

[115] Examples might include social class, language, race, national origins, education, age, preferences in music, marital status, and health. Church growth movement scholars have used the term, "homogeneous unit principle" to refer to such an emphasis.

[116] Schaller, 1994:111.

[117] Schaller, 1994:84,85.

[118] Wagner 1984:186.

[119] Bert Witvoet, in the *Christian Courier*, January 27, 1995:4

[120] The following material is drawn from Wagner, 1984:104 and Towns, 1990:43-58;73-88.

[121] Towns, 1990:77.

[122] Source: *Dominion Magazine*, Summer 1993:5-9

[123] Towns, 1990:11.

[124] Webster, 1992:16-17.

[125] Hauerwas and Willimon, 1989:12.

[126] Campolo, 1991:115-116.

[127] See, for example, *Unitrends*, pp. 74ff.

[128] Towns, 1990:51.

References

Anderson, Leith, *A Church for the 21st Century* (Minneapolis: Bethany House, 1992)

Barna, George, *Marketing the Church* (Colorado Springs: Navpress, 1988).
——*User Friendly Churches* (Ventura, Calif.: Regal Books, 1991)

Bellah, Robert, Richard Madsen, William Sullivan, Ann Swidler, and Steven Tipton, *Habits of the Heart* (New York: Harper and Row, 1985)

Berger, Peter L., *Invitation to Sociology* (New York: Doubleday, 1963)

Best, Marion and friends, *Will Our Church Disappear? Strategies for the Renewal of The United Church of Canada* (Winfield, B.C.: Wood Lake Books, 1994)

Bibby, Reginald W., *Anglitrends* (Toronto: Anglican Diocese, 1986)
——*Fragmented Gods: the Poverty and Potential of Religion of Canada* (Toronto: Stoddart, 1987)
——*Mosaic Madness: Pluralism Without A Cause* (Toronto: Stoddart, 1990).
——*Unknown Gods: the Ongoing Story of Religion in Canada* (Toronto: Stoddart, 1993)
——*Unitrends* (Toronto: Department of Stewardship Services, United Church of Canada, 1994)
——"Going, Going Gone: The Impact of Geographical Mobility on Religious Involvement in Canada," *Review of Religious Research*, 1995, in press

Bibby, Reginald W. and Merlin B. Brinkerhoff, "Circulation of the Saints, 1966-1990: New Data, New Reflections," *Journal for the Scientific Study of Religion* 33:273-280, 1994.

Bibby, Reginald W. and Donald C. Posterski, *The Emerging Generation: An Inside Look at Canada's Teenagers* (Toronto: Irwin, 1985)
——*Teen Trends: A Nation in Motion* (Toronto: Stoddart, 1992)

Campolo, Tony, *Wake Up America!* (San Francisco: Harper 1991)

Canadian Conference of Catholic Bishops, *Pathways to Faithfulness: Developing Structures Which Support Catechetical Ministry With Adults* (Ottawa: Publications Service, CCCB, 1993)

Caplovitz, David and Fred Sherrow, *The Religious Drop-Outs: Apostasy Among College Graduates* (Beverly Hills, CA: Sage, 1977)

Dudley, Carl S. (ed), *Building Effective Ministry: Theory and Practice in the Local Church* (San Francisco: Harper and Row, 1983)

Easum, Bill, *Dancing With Dinosaurs* (Nashville: Abingdon, 1993)

Finke, Roger and Rodney Stark, *The Churching of America, 1976-1990* (Rutgers, NJ: Rutgers University Press, 1992)

Freud, Sigmund, *The Future of An Illusion* (New York: Doubleday, 1962)

Fraser, Brian J., *Fire in the Sanctuary: Leadership in the Presbyterian Church in Canada* (Vancouver: St. Andrew's Hall, 1993)

Hadaway, C. Kirk, *What Can We Do About Church Dropouts?* (Nashville: Abingdon, 1990)
——*Church Growth Principles: Separating Fact from Fiction* (Nashville: Broadman Press, 1991)
——and Penny Long Marler, "All in the Family: Religious Mobility in America," *Review of Religious Research* 35:97-116, 1993)
——and David A. Roozen, *Rerouting the Protestant Mainstream: Sources of Growth and Opportunities for Change* (Nashville: Abingdon, 1995),

Hunsberger, Bruce, "A Reexamination of the Antecendents of Apostasy," *Review of Religious Research* 21:158-170, 1980
——"Apostasy: A Social Learning Perspective," *Review of Religious Research* 25:21-38, 1983

Hauerwas, Stanley and William H. Willimon, *Resident Aliens* (Nashville: Abingdon, 1989

Johnson, Douglas W., *Vitality Means Church Growth* (Nashville: Abingdon, 1989).

Kawano, Roland M., *The Global City: Multicultural Ministry in Urban Canada* (Winfield, B.C.: Wood Lake Books, 1992)

Marler, Penny Long and C. Kirk Hadway, "Toward A Typology of 'Marginal Members'," *Review of Religious Research* 35:34-54, 1993

Maus, Armand L., "Dimensions of Religious Defection," *Review of Religious Research* 10:128-135.
——*The Angel and the Beehive: The Mormon Struggle With Assimilation* (Urbana/Chicago: University of Illinois Press, 1994)

Mead, Loren B., *The Once and Future Church: Reinventing the Congregation for a New Mission Frontier* (Washington: The Alban Institute, 1991)
——*Transforming Congregations for the Future* (Washington: The Alban Institute, 1994)

Miller, Herb, *The Vital Congregation* (Nashville: Abingdon, 1990)

Motz, Arnell, *Reclaiming a Nation* (Richmond, B.C., Church Leadership Library, 1990

Nash, Dennison and Peter L. Berger, "The Child, the Family, and the 'Religious Revival' in Suburbia," *Journal for the Scientific Study of Religion,* 2:85-93, 1962

Ozark, Elisabeth Weiss, "Social and Cognitive Influences on the Development of Religious Beliefs and Commitment in Adolescence," *Journal for the Scientific Study of Religion* 28:448-463, 1989

Parsons, Talcott, "Christianity and Modern Industrial Society," in Edward Teryakian (ed.), *Sociocultural Theory, Values, and Sociocultural Change* (Glencoe, Ill.: The Free Press, 1963)

Posterski, Donald C. and Irwin Barker, *Where's a Good Church?* (Winfield, B.C.: Wood Lake Books, 1993)

Roof, Wade Clark, *A Generation of Seekers* (San Francisco: Harper, 1993)
——and William McKinney, *American Mainline Religion* (New Brunswick, NJ: Rutgers University Press, 1987)

Roozen, David A., William McKinney, and Wayne Thompson, "The 'Big Chill' Generation Warms Up to Worship," *Review of Religious Research* 31:314-322

Roxburgh, Alan J., *Reaching a New Generation* (Downers Grove, Illinois: InterVarsity Press, 1993

Russell, Letty M., *Church in the Road: Feminist Interpretation of the Church* (Louisville: Westminster/John Knox Press, 1993)

Schaller, Lyle E., *Innovations in Ministry: Models for the 21st Century* (Nashville: Abingdon, 1994)

Smith, Glenn, "Reaching Canada's Cities for Christ," in *Urban Mission* 8:27-36, 1990

Steele, Pat, "Growing Churches in Canada," in *Dominion Magazine* 1:5-9, 1993

Stiller, Brian C., *Critical Options for Evangelicals* (Markham, Ontario: Faith Today Publications, 1991)

Towns, Elmer L., *10 of Today's Most Innovative Churches* (Ventura, Calif.: Regal Books, 1990

Ward, Kenn, *This Evangelical Lutheran Church of Ours* (Winfield, B.C.: Wood Lake Books, 1994)

Webster, Douglas D., *Selling Jesus: What's Wrong With Marketing the Church.* (Downers Grove, Illinois: InterVarsity Press, 1992)

*Also by Reginald Bibby
and available from Wood Lake Books...*

Fragmented Gods
by Reginald W. Bibby
ISBN 0-7737-54229
· $15.95

Unknown Gods
The Ongoing Story of Religion in Canada
by Reginald W. Bibby
ISBN 0-7737-5606X
· $18.95

Mosaic Madness
by Reginald W. Bibby
ISBN 0-7737-53990
· $15.95

The Emerging Generation
An Inside Look at Canada's Teenagers
by Reginald W. Bibby & Don Posterski
ISBN 0-7725-18181
· $12.95

Teen Trends
New Directions, New Responses
by Reginald W. Bibby & Don Posterski
ISBN 0-7737-55314
· $17.95

To order: Contact your local bookstore or call Wood Lake Books

In Canada phone 1-800-663-2775   Fax: 604-766-2736
Outside Canada phone 604-766-2778   Office hours: 8:00 a.m.–4:30 p.m. Pacific Time